REVOLUTION IN

EASTERN EUROPE

*Understanding the Collapse of
Communism in Poland, Hungary,
East Germany, Czechoslovakia,
Romania, and the Soviet Union*

Peter Cipkowski

John Wiley & Sons, Inc.

New York • Chichester • Brisbane • Toronto • Singapore

In recognition of the importance of preserving what has been written, it is a policy of John Wiley & Sons, Inc., to have books of enduring value published in the United States printed on acid-free paper, and we exert our best efforts to that end.

Library of Congress Cataloging in Publication Data

Cipkowski, Peter
    Revolution in Eastern Europe: understanding the collapse of communism in Poland, Hungary, East Germany, Czechoslovakia, Romania, and the Soviet Union / by Peter Cipkowski
    p.   cm. — (Our changing world)
    Includes bibliographical references.
    Summary: Analyzes the fall of communism in Eastern Europe, country by country, during 1989 and 1990. Includes photographs, time lines, maps, and cartoons.
    ISBN 0-471-53967-8 (libr. ed.)   ISBN 0-471-53968-6 (pbk.)
    1. European, Eastern—Politics and government—1989-   [1. Europe, Eastern—Politics and government—1989-   ]   I. Title.   II. Series: Our changing world (New York, N.Y.)
DJK51.C57   1991
940'.09717—dc20   90-26990
                                                                          CIP
                                                                          AC

Printed in the United States of America
91 90 10 9 8 7 6 5 4 3 2 1

Contents

Acknowledgments

Many individuals have helped me at various times with encouragement, discussion, ideas, and criticism. Among them, I want to thank Mark Cawley and Martin Blais for their friendship and valuable input. I am also grateful to Katherine Cornell who gave selflessly and cheerfully of her time, energy, and knowledge. Her interpretation of the events in Eastern Europe and commitment to her own book project sharpened my interest in the region. Natalie Goldstein introduced me to the complex world of photo agencies; when I invoked her name, a door was opened. Roger Scholl was an extremely patient editor; without his care, this book would otherwise be much more defective than it is. Finally, it remains to thank my friend, Steve Ross, who first suggested I write about Eastern Europe and encouraged me along the way. Without him, this book would never have been completed.

The purpose of this book is to provide a general overview of the dramatic events that took place in Eastern Europe in 1989. Throughout it, I have freely quoted from scholars, journalists, and witnesses. Quite frequently, I have not identified the source. In an attempt to avoid overburdening the text with names, I have included the identities of only the most central figures in the story of the Revolution of 1989. I am sure that some readers will find the absence of bibliographic references to be a frustrating defect. I have, however, provided at the end of the book a suggested reading list for those interested in reading further.

INTRODUCTION

Sweeping Change

In EASTERN EUROPE, 1989 was a year of sweeping change. One must to go back to 1945, the year Germany and Japan were defeated in World War II, to find the last time the world stood on the threshold of such an entirely new era. In 1989, forty years of history began to be challenged in a few months. The people of Eastern Europe started a revolution, the world's largest empire crumbled, and this century's longest war—the Cold War—came to a close.

The trouble with reform

The 19th-century French philosopher Alexis de Tocqueville once wrote, "The most dangerous time for a bad government is when it starts to reform." These words might well have been ringing around the world in 1989. Mikhail Gorbachev, leader of the Soviet Union, was in the process of reforming the failing Communist system. Suddenly, something gave way. On the fringes of the Soviet empire, people started taking back the freedom withheld from them for generations.

In the beginning of 1989, on the eve of the Communist collapse, the countries of Eastern Europe were still entrenched in a Soviet empire. Their governments were run by members of Communist parties that looked to Moscow for support. By the end of 1989, the totalitarian leaders of Poland, Hungary, East Germany, Czechoslovakia, and Romania had been removed from power. The transformation was most advanced in Poland. There, former political prisoners had already been in power for more than three months. Hungary was not far behind; its reform-minded Communists were preparing for Hungary's first totally free election since 1945. The wall that disfigured the border between the two Germanys—and sliced the city of Berlin in two—suddenly became irrelevant as the desperate East German regime punched holes in it to allow free passage in both directions. The hard-line Communist leadership of East Germany collapsed, stirring up the possibility of German reunification that set off alarms in all the capitals of Europe. In Prague, a dissident playwright personally guided members of the Communist party out of their offices, down the corridor, and out the door. Finally, on Christmas Day 1989, Romania's brutal Communist dictator was executed after days of bloody uprisings, increasing hopes for the rebirth of democracy there.

Revolution

The events of 1989 were revolutionary. In revolutions, those who were at the bottom suddenly ascend to the top. Prisoners take charge of the police, stokers become foreign ministers. Revolution turned things around in Eastern Europe in 1989, but with three crucial differences. First, except for Romania, these changes were accomplished without violence. Second, some of those who were previously on top were left on top. Third, those who were, until the revolution, left on the bottom would, under normal conditions in democratic countries, never have been at the bottom at all.

For example, Jiri Dienstbier stoked coal into a factory furnace until his appointment as foreign minister of Czechoslovakia in early December 1989. Under a non-Communist system, he might have been a senior editor at a newspaper, as journalism was his original career. But his career was interrupted when the Soviets invaded Czechoslovakia in 1968. Similarly, Jan Carnogursky was a prisoner until December 1989; he is now deputy premier with responsibility for Czechoslovakia's security apparatus. But as a distinguished Slovak lawyer he might, under a non-Communist system, have already played a leading role in the government of his country. So the revolution of 1989 did not so much "turn the world upside down"; instead it led the world toward a new, democratic order.

The legacy of Yalta

To understand how Eastern Europe lost its democratic order, one must return to 1945, the last year of World War II. In that year, the American, British, and French troops were fighting the last battles of the war against the Germans in western Europe. In the

Joseph Stalin, general secretary of the Soviet Union, and British Prime Minister Winston Churchill at the Yalta Conference in 1945. (AP, Wide World Photos)

east, Stalin's Red Army had already "liberated" Warsaw, Budapest, Prague, and Bucharest. In February, victory in Europe was more or less assured for the Allies, so U.S. President Franklin Roosevelt, Britain's Prime Minister Winston Churchill, and Soviet leader Joseph Stalin met at Yalta, a Russian resort on the Black Sea, to discuss "a strategy of peace." After years of war, Europe was devastated.

One of the first problems the leaders discussed was how to deal with Germany after its defeat. Should the nation be divided among the victors? Should the Germans be allowed to pick up where they had left off before the war began? The Allied leaders decided that Germany as well as the city of Berlin would be divided into four temporary occupation zones. Each of these zones would be controlled separately by France, Great Britain, the United States, and the Soviet Union.

The most difficult problem for the Allies, however, was the control of the region east of the Elbe River. By the time of the Yalta conference, the Soviet army was only 40 miles from Berlin. The Soviets had successfully crushed the German armies throughout the east. Roosevelt and Churchill feared that Stalin would incorporate these "liberated" lands into his empire. They insisted at Yalta that Stalin give assurances that this would not happen. Stalin gave his word. He promised that the countries would be completely independent and that free elections would be held as soon as possible. By July 1945, however, it was clear that Stalin had lied. In a telegram to Churchill, Stalin declared that "a freely elected government in any of these eastern European countries would be anti-Soviet, and *that* we could not allow."

The beginning of a Cold War

So began the Cold War. Shortly after World War II, the world became polarized between two opposing camps. One group of nations—the West—included the United States, Great Britain, France, and most other democracies of Western Europe. The other group—the Eastern, or Soviet bloc—included the Soviet Union and the nations of Eastern Europe that came under Soviet control in the last year of the war. The Cold War was a state of tension and hostility between the non-Communist nations of the West and the Eastern bloc countries. The ideological struggle between capitalism and communism was at the heart of the conflict.

Relations between the West and the Eastern bloc strained as it grew apparent that the Soviets did not intend to relinquish control of the Eastern European countries. The Cold War grew out of long-held distrust between East and West. Soviet leaders had never forgotten that Western nations helped anti-Bolshevik forces in 1917 during the Russian Revolution. The Soviets also resented the Allies' prewar policy of "see nothing, say nothing" toward Hitler, which had allowed him to gain control of lands within striking distance of the Soviet Union. After the Germans invaded the Soviet Union in 1941, the Soviets felt that the Allies' refusal to open a second front had left the Soviet people bearing most of the burden of the war.

Western leaders, on the other hand, believed that the Soviet Union's 1939 nonaggression pact with Germany, in which they agreed to divide Poland down the middle, created "the atmosphere of war." The Hitler-Stalin Pact encouraged the German invasion of Poland on September 1, 1939, and set off the war. Moreover, Western powers saw the Soviets as leaders of a worldwide Communist movement that aimed to spread revolution and destroy democracy. Soviet-backed Communist parties were already shaping the Eastern bloc nations into satellites. The intent of the Soviet Union was to create Communist-dominated coalition governments, closely bound to the Soviet Union.

An iron curtain

In March 1946, Winston Churchill sadly described the new separation of Europe: "From Stettin in the Baltic to Trieste in the Adriatic, an iron curtain has descended across the continent. Behind that line lie all the capitals of the ancient states of Central and Eastern Europe. . . . These famous cities and the populations around them lie in what I must call the Soviet sphere, and all are subject . . . to an increasing measure of control from Moscow."

Churchill's words so aptly described the situation that "iron curtain" became the term used for the sharp division between the Soviet bloc and the West.

By 1948, Communist governments had been imposed by Stalin in Albania, Bulgaria, Romania, Poland, Hungary, and Czechoslovakia. Later that year, cold war tensions erupted in Germany. As they agreed at Yalta, each of the wartime Allies occupied one area of Germany. Delays in signing the treaty and other disagreements soon complicated this joint control. The Western nations realized that it was important for the Germans to be included in long-range plans. Moreover, the United States, Great Britain, and France planned to merge their three major occupation zones and turn over control to a new government run by Germans. Fearful of German resurgence, however, the Soviet Union objected, and the four-power council could not come to an agreement. To put pressure on the West, the Soviets shut off all land routes to Berlin from their zone of Germany, effectively isolating Berlin within Soviet-held territory. Like Germany, Berlin had been divided into four sectors, and the three Allies now had to find a way to provide support for their parts of the city.

In response to the plight of the Berliners, the United States organized a massive airlift to bring food, coal, and other supplies to the city's 2.5 million people. A year later, having failed to achieve their goals, the Soviets finally lifted the blockade, but Germany and Berlin remained split between East and West. West Berlin continued to be isolated inside Communist territory. Almost immediately, a new constitution created a democratic government for the Federal Republic of Germany, or West Germany, the former Allied Zone. A few months later, the Soviet-held territory became the German Democratic Republic, or East Germany.

The Stalinization of Eastern Europe

The new Communist-dominated regimes introduced massive reforms. For example, governments confiscated and redistributed thousands of large family farms. They put uncultivated land to use so that more than three million peasant families acquired about six million acres of land. The reforms effectively ended the landed aristocracy that once dominated the countries of Eastern Europe. The new regimes, taking advantage of the fact that many of their prewar industries were owned by foreigners or run by pro-German collaborators, also nationalized much of the economy. Struggling with the burden of postwar reconstruction, they even lent a sympathetic ear to receiving American aid. But Stalin was not disposed to permit these countries to drift into the Western economic orbit. Nor did he view favorably the growing strength of the small landowners or the cries for free elections in which the Communists could lose their hold.

By 1948, wherever non-Communist elements were still strong, the Communists ousted their political rivals, banned, or reduced to powerlessness, all other political parties, and set up single-party Communist regimes. The governments were styled as "people's democracies." In Czechoslovakia, liberal leaders like Eduard Benes and Jan Masaryk hoped for a time that their country would serve as a bridge between Soviets and the West. There the coalition government lasted longer than elsewhere, but ended in a Communist coup in February 1948 and the death of Masaryk.

With the Communists in complete control, many leaders of opposition movements were exiled, imprisoned, or in other ways silenced. The people's democracies also clashed with religious groups, especially the Roman Catholic Church; high-ranking prelates were denounced, brought to public trial, and imprisoned, and Church property was confiscated.

As in the Russian Revolution, the Communist leaders themselves became victims. From 1949 to 1953, reflecting the tightening repression in the Soviet Union itself in Stalin's last years, the familiar pattern of purges, arrests, trials, confessions, and executions occurred in the highest ranks of each party.

After Stalin's death in 1953, many Eastern European governments, including the Soviet Union, engineered somewhat phony eras of "de-Stalinization." Stalin was renounced at the Twentieth Party Congress in February 1956. Nikita Khrushchev, the new general secretary of the Soviet Communist party, delivered a sensational speech. Among other things, the new leader admitted that under Stalin there had been "monstrous" and "gross violations of

A victim of the Cold War lying beside the Berlin Wall.
Scores of East Germans were killed by the Communist
border guards while trying to escape to West Berlin in the
1960s and 1970s. (Reuters/Bettmann Archives)

the basic Leninist principles." Nonetheless, Khrushchev's government did very little to correct the dictator's mistakes. As a result,
Stalin's totalitarian policies remained intact. In Poland, Hungary,
and Czechoslovakia, the de-Stalinization program opened a Pan-

dora's box; destroying Stalin's infallibility destroyed Soviet infallibility as well. In 1956, 1968, 1970, 1976, and 1980, Eastern Europeans marched in the streets, demanded more freedom, and condemned the Soviet occupation of their countries. Each attempt to loosen the Soviet Union's control was crushed.

Mikhail Gorbachev

Until 1989, the people of Eastern Europe lived under communism's totalitarian grip. They lacked even the most basic human rights. They were not allowed to criticize the government. There was no way for them to present alternative candidates for government posts. There was no free press. They could not practice their religion. They could not travel.

Then, quite unexpectedly, the grip was loosened. The iron curtain began to crumble.

At the center of revolutions in Eastern Europe stood the extraordinary figure of Mikhail Gorbachev, the leader of the Soviet Union. The revolutions owe a great deal to his initiative and his acknowledgment of communism's decay. When Gorbachev was elected general secretary of the Soviet Communist party in March 1985, he admitted that the problems of the Soviet Union "were poised to generate catastrophic and possibly irreversible damages." Moreover, Gorbachev expressed his concern that the system lacked integrity and the moral support of the people.

The Soviet Union's colossal military power rivaled the military strength of the United States. Nonetheless, it had been in economic, political, and moral decline for decades. For the Soviet Union to maintain its superpower status, Gorbachev and his supporters felt it was necessary to remove the accretions of the past. The new leader introduced two words to the vocabulary of communism: *perestroika* and *glasnost*. *Perestroika,* or restructuring, set into motion a massive overhaul of economic policies. *Glasnost,* or openness, invited people to talk more freely about the nation's problems and about finding solutions. These two words would soon have a profound effect on the course of modern history.

In his 1988 speech before the United Nations General As-

The Communist leaders of the Warsaw Pact, before the revolutions of 1989. *Left to right*: Erich Honecker, East Germany; Milos Jakes, Czechoslovakia; Mikhail Gorbachev, Soviet Union; Wojciech Jaruzelski, Poland; Nicolae Ceausescu, Romania; Todor Zhivkov, Bulgaria; and Rezso Nyers, Hungary. (CAF/Warszawa)

sembly, Gorbachev signaled another important change. The subject peoples of Stalin's empire were free to go their own ways. "Freedom of choice," Gorbachev said, "is a universal principle which allows no exceptions." In early 1989, at the annual meeting of Eastern Europe's leaders, Gorbachev proclaimed a policy of nonintervention. The official statement said: "No country has the right to dictate events in another country, to assume the position of judge or arbiter."

Poland and Hungary were the first Eastern bloc nations to take the Soviet president at his word. They abandoned the Leninist principle that Communist parties must forever play the leading role in society. Both countries made history by allowing their citizens to register their rejection of Communism at the ballot box. When Moscow raised no objection, the people of East Germany and

Czechoslovakia moved quickly to end the Communists' power monopoly in their countries.

Still, it was astonishing that the Soviet Union would stand by and watch its empire unravel. Many scholars have explained what happened by noting that the nations of Eastern Europe were becoming a drain on Soviet economic and military resources. Although Gorbachev was not disposed to dismantle the Soviet bloc on short notice, he acknowledged that change was inevitable, even in the sphere of military arrangements. "Life changes, and this alliance, too, will be transformed," he said at the Warsaw Pact summit conference in July 1988. "Alliances are not forever."

Alliances are not forever

Eastern Europe is "a great territory of unanswered questions and unresolved contradictions," the German philosopher and historian Bruno Bauer wrote in 1854. So it remains. And of those unresolved contradictions, none was greater than the region's self-evident longing for democracy. If the events of 1989 have been surprising—if they have outdistanced and exceeded all expectations—they say almost nothing about what the future will hold. The transition from what had seemed permanent cold war conditions is still underway. What will happen through the 1990s in these separate societies is unknown. The good news—the end of the Cold War—is often obscured by the general confusion of most new governments and the economic hardships that still exist in Eastern Europe. With no compass, the various non-Communist helmsmen, as we will see, may not be sure how to create stable democracies.

POLAND

A Pact for Democracy

Thousands of pro-Solidarity demonstrators routinely gathered
in the streets of Poland throughout the 1980s, carrying
banners and chanting anti-Communist slogans.
(CAF/Warszawa)

A Chronology of Events in Poland

February 1945	Poland's postwar fate is decided at Yalta.
January 1947	The Communist party gains control.
June 1956	Strikes break out in Poznan; 57 people are killed.
March 1968	Student riots take place in Warsaw.
December 1970	Riots and strikes occur in Polish coastal cities; more than three hundred are reported killed.
October 16, 1978	Cardinal Karol Wojtyla of Krakow is elected Pope, taking the name John Paul II.
August 1980	Eighty thousand workers take over the Lenin Shipyard in Gdansk; strikes break out throughout the country.
August 31, 1980	Poland's Communist government signs agreement with strike committee in Gdansk; Solidarity era begins.
December 13, 1981	Martial law is imposed; Solidarity is banned; thousands are imprisoned.
May/August 1988	Massive strikes break out across the country; on both occasions, strikers demand restoration of Solidarity.
February 6, 1989	First "roundtable" meeting takes place between government and Solidarity.

April 7, 1989	Government agress to relegalize Solidarity and hold partly free elections.
June 4, 1989	Solidarity candidates triumph in Eastern Europe's freest elections ever held under Communist rule.
August 24, 1989	Tadeusz Mazowiecki is confirmed as prime minister and forms the first non-Communist government in Eastern Europe since 1948.
January 1, 1990	Introduction of fundamental economic reforms, securing a market system.
May 27, 1990	Local elections sweep away Communist officials throughout the country.
December 9, 1990	In Poland's first free election since 1947, Lech Walesa is elected president, winning 75 percent of the vote.

DURING THE FIRST PART of 1989, a new, strange light appeared in Poland. It illuminated the world in an unexpected way. An eerie sentence written by Winston Churchill in about 1914 received a new meaning: "And a strange light began immediately, but by perceptible gradations, to fall and grow upon the map of Europe." The strange light that Churchill referred to in 1914 was the glimmering advent of World War I. The strange light in 1989 revealed the fatal loosening of communism in Eastern Europe.

Poland's metamorphosis

The year 1989 was one of enormous importance, as changes unthinkable a year earlier now occurred with dizzying speed. In Poland, the collapse of communism is a story of a remarkable coming-together, for almost no one imagined that the great gulf between the government and the people could be so swiftly bridged. Many details of this "bridge" are still obscure, as they are for each of the ongoing revolutions in Eastern Europe. But two things are clear. First, it would not have been possible without the explicit permission of Soviet leader Mikhail Gorbachev. Second, the essential revolutionary jolt was provided by two waves of strikes in May and August 1988. The second wave was larger than the first, and resulted in the restoration of a banned trade union called Solidarity.

Agreements signed in April 1989 by the Communist government and Solidarity led to monumental constitutional changes. They included the call for Eastern Europe's freest parliamentary election since the end of World War II. Given this unique chance to cast a vote, the Polish people voted overwhelmingly against the Communist party. With the Soviet Union's acquiescence, Solidarity formed Eastern Europe's first non-Communist government. Nonetheless, the Polish opposition suddenly found themselves thrust into an unenviable position. They now must initiate highly unpopular economic reforms or take the blame for economic failure. Meanwhile, the Communist party has quietly stepped into the shadows, and has ceased to exist in its old form.

Russophobia

The opposition movement in Poland was always slightly more constant and steady than it was elsewhere in Eastern Europe. In Poland, the loosening of communism had been going on for many decades.

Poland's postwar fate was decided at Yalta by the Allied powers, against the will of the Polish people. Both politically and militarily, Poland was the first country to resist Nazi aggression in World War II. Consistently, and on a truly massive scale, the country engaged itself on the Allies' side. Because of this, Polish leaders believed the Allied promises to rebuild an independent Polish state. Poland, however, was central to Soviet policy in Europe. Only with Poland's full subordination to the Soviet Union could Stalin realize his plans to create a Soviet bloc. Stalin broke his promise at the Yalta conference for "free and unfettered elections" in Poland. The election of January 1947, accompanied by terror and lies, was rigged. Through these corrupted "elections," the Soviet Union imposed Communist rule in Poland.

For many centuries, Polish-Russian relations had been marked by great hostility. Moscow's expansion to the west from the 17th to the 19th centuries took place at the expense of the Polish commonwealth; tsarist Russia launched the destruction of the independent Polish nation, erasing it from the map of Europe in 1795. Generations of Poles came of age with an internal awareness of their national identity, and with a strong desire for independence from the Russian aggressor. Soviet control over Poland was made particularly repugnant by their historical antagonism, combined with their experiences in World War II: the Hitler-Stalin pact of 1939 and the ensuing invasion of Poland by the Soviet army on September 17, 1939; the mass deportation of Poles from Polish lands; and the Katyn forest massacre of several thousand Polish officers by the Soviet army.

The reaction of Polish society toward the new political order was understandably bitter. There was a feeling of resignation, as well, stemming from the fact that Poland had been deserted by its Western allies. The terrible injustice of Allied and Soviet decisions made at Yalta, the memory of the Katyn massacre, the agony of the war—fought in complete isolation—could never be erased from the Poles' consciousness. They had been left to make the most of life under communism.

1956, 1968, 1970, 1976

Violent clashes soon erupted between the Polish people and their Communist authorities. A common sight in many Polish cities was graffiti on the sides of buildings listing the years of upheaval in Poland: 1956, 1968, 1970, and 1976. In each year, there had been courageous explosions against the Communist regime. This simple list carried an extremely potent message: Rise up and do it again.

There is a rhythm in the series of political crises that have taken place in Communist Poland. In 1956, workers in Poznan were crushed when they protested the government's unwillingness to "de-Stalinize." The year 1968 brought a new wave of bloody student riots in Warsaw. In 1970, workers' unrest broke out in the Baltic port cities of Gdansk, Gydnia, and Sopot. In all these strikes, including those that erupted in Radom and Warsaw in 1976, there was a lack of unity among the strikers. Each was ended by the government's use of brutal force. Despite promises to make changes, the Party leadership returned to its old pattern of rule as soon as the immediate crisis passed. The Communist leaders went back to their Central Committee building and devised yet another demoralizing strategy—one that would safeguard the Party's monopoly on power.

After 1976, Polish dissidents went beyond the previous bounds of dissent. They set up institutions that were completely out of place in a totalitarian society. They established a "flying university," which moved from place to place, offering a large variety of courses unavailable at the government universities. They started numerous publications, some of which were published on a regular basis and had devoted readers. They founded a committee to defend workers against harassment and unjust imprisonment by the government. Of course, most of these activities were conducted "underground," in secret. According to a close observer of the Polish scene, the Poles established a measure of freedom by simply acting like free people. At the same time, they were teaching the world what striving for freedom ultimately is about: not riot and insurrection, but the right to peacefully attend to one's own business and the business of one's society.

1980—the Polish August

In the summer of 1980, the Polish government announced price increases that would affect meat products. In an attempt to avoid sudden, mass unrest, further price changes were to be staggered, affecting different parts of the country at different times. By August, strikes spread throughout the country as workers demanded higher salaries to compensate for the increase in prices.

By mid-August 1980, the strikers in Gdansk captured world attention. The unique feature of the Gdansk strikers was their ability to organize themselves. Much of this had to do with an

The world's attention focused on the gates of Lenin Shipyard in Gdansk during 1980. Outside the gates, supporters of the workers rallied daily. As a result of this strike, the Solidarity movement was born. (CAF/Warszawa)

ordinary Polish citizen, an electrician named Lech Walesa. As the strikers in the Lenin Shipyard gathered, Walesa climbed its 12-foot-high gates, grabbed a microphone, and became their leader. He was already a familiar face and was known for his sharp opinions, which often contradicted those of the Communist government. The shipyard bureaucracy had left him feeling "frustrated for years." What set him apart was his genius for expressing his frustrations and creating a concrete response to them. He was a natural leader whose confidence inspired the workers. Even Walesa was surprised by his ability to publicly challenge the Communist authorities. "I was trembling with anger when I climbed the gate," Walesa explained. "I was sickened by the lies and the mediocrity of the Communist leadership. There was no time to think that I was risking my life. That came later."

The workers' requests were straightforward. They demanded more civil liberties, higher wages, at least one day off a week, more day-care nurseries, the right to strike, and the right to criticize the management without risk of being fired. Walesa told one reporter that the government "has to grant our wishes if they want to continue to govern, because the workers will go on striking for five years." Faced with so fierce a show of opposition, the Polish regime backed down. On August 31, 1980, the government signed an agreement with the strikers. The agreement granted their requests and permitted the establishment of the free trade union Solidarity.

The era of Solidarity

Through an independent, self-governing trade union, Polish workers took control of their future. Millions of people, living in neighboring Communist nations, watched enviously. For the next 15 months, Solidarity blossomed into an umbrella group of workers, intellectuals, students, and farmers. It guided more than 50 unions and more than ten million members. It exercised free speech and published several newspapers.

The Solidarity era was a culmination of a long series of hopeful events in Poland. Unlike the upheavals of 1956, 1968, 1970, and 1976, however, the uprising of August 1980 was a breakthrough. As in 1970 and 1976, the real movement began among the working class. In 1980, however, Polish workers showed a political wisdom that had not been present before. By acting and speaking with a combination of courage and restraint, they loosened their government's totalitarian grip.

Some historians call the Solidarity era Poland's "self-limiting revolution." It was called self-limiting because, although it enjoyed the overwhelming support of the Polish public, it held back from attempting to overthrow the government. The movement enjoyed the crucial full-scale participation of the working class and formed an alliance with the Catholic Church, which has always been a powerful influence in Polish society. There was dedication to liberty and to the movement's internal democracy. Though schooled in opposition to totalitarian rule, the Polish self-limiting revolution did not grow to react to or mimic its bullying opponent. Its answer to totalitarian violence and deception was not violence and deception, but non-violence and openness.

Martial law

Within months of Solidarity's founding, the Polish Communist party lost more than one-fourth of its total membership. By December 1981, the Communist leadership had had enough. In the early hours of December 13, a Communist-backed military junta slammed the door on democracy, and Poland's first experiment with democracy since World War II came to a halt—or postponement. For the next 20 months, Poland was led by its own army.

Addressing the nation on Sunday morning, December 13, General Wojciech Jaruzelski announced that he was the head of the Military Council of National Salvation. He emphasized that he was speaking as a military man and as the head of government. He did not mention the Communist party, which he also led. General Jaruzelski explained that during the night hundreds of arrests had been made throughout the country. More would follow. He added that he was counting on the cooperation of all "socialist Poland." The nation, he said, would once again "resume its peaceful and Communist destiny."

Poland's army takeover was similar to a military coup, including a declaration of martial law, mass internments, seizure of the communications network, public harassment, and strict censorship. But it lacked one significant ingredient of a military coup—it was aimed not at overthrowing the existing power, but rather at destroying the opposition that had been challenging the Party's monopoly for more than 14 months.

In effect, the Communist-backed military intervened to fill a political vacuum left by the collapse of Communist political authority. But Solidarity's chapter was not closed on December 13. Although Walesa was imprisoned, along with scores of other Solidarity leaders, angry citizens gathered in protest in the streets. The authorities responded by sending huge squads of *zomos*, ruthless storm troopers, to break up the demonstrations. Protesters were beaten indiscriminately by the *zomos*; tear gas exploded in schoolyards; water canons trapped old women against walls; and *zomos* truncheons pummeled the skulls of innocent bystanders.

But Polish citizens already sampled freedom; in fact, they had never been so free. During the dismal years that followed the upheavels of 1981, most of Poland lived with the memory of that freedom. The power of their resistance to enslavement, combined with the imagination of the workers and intellectuals among them, would bring about even more historic changes in 1989. Not only would Solidarity be reborn, but Poland would be returned to the democratic institutions of Europe.

The Party's crisis of faith

After imposing martial law, Poland's Communist leaders began to lose faith in themselves. It appeared, as many would later admit, that the Party was often divided on how to enforce martial law. After years of repeated economic failures and political repression, Poland's unpopular leaders were apparently concluding that they could not govern the country without the people's support. According to Mieczyslaw Rakowski, Poland's former Communist prime minister, the Party was going through a "crisis of faith." He said, "We needed a new definition of socialism. It was sure to take many years but it was essential to give the concept fresh meaning. I was sure that nobody in Poland was ready to go to the barricades, including the Communists, so I thought we had time."

The Communist retreat started in August 1988. Neither the government nor Solidarity had a credible program for dealing with the problems of an exhausted, virtually bankrupt nation. Solidarity membership had dwindled. It was no longer a mass movement. The union's diminished ranks were torn by disagreements, and a wave of angry strikes, mostly unauthorized, was creating havoc in the economy. The two sides finally realized that each needed the other to share the responsibility—and the blame—for a long-delayed effort to turn the economy around, an effort that would demand heavy sacrifices from the people. Walesa, whose appeals for talks with the government had been rejected till then, played his cards shrewdly. Most Poles, he said, did not "care a fig about Walesa or

Solidarity," but they would support the union movement as long as the government persisted in governing alone and in making people's lives miserable. The regime's pollster agreed. He wrote in a Warsaw newspaper article that the government's own "bumbling" was responsible for the worrying round of August strikes, the second in four months. Something had to be done.

It started with a meeting in a Warsaw suburb between Walesa and General Czeslaw Kiszczak, the interior minister. Only seven years earlier, General Kiszczak had signed the martial-law order that led to Walesa's 11-month imprisonment. Now the interior minister had an astonishing proposal: If Walesa could persuade the strikers to go back to work, the regime would consider restoring Solidarity's legal status as an independent union. The stakes were high. If Walesa succeeded in ending the strikes, the government would have to negotiate with the union it had outlawed and somehow failed to destroy. If he failed, Walesa and Solidarity would have lost considerable integrity.

Within three days, Walesa halted the strikes—and promptly found himself accused of capitulation by many angry younger workers. But Walesa, whose courage and instinctive political skills had seen him through more difficult moments, defended his leadership at a post-strike rally in Gdansk with a self-confidence bordering on arrogance. "I have not been a traitor and I will not be a traitor," he said. "You wanted more than I could deliver, especially my adversaries. But I am not going to toy with Poland. I extinguished the strikes and I will extinguish any others that happen." Walesa had long believed, and Kiszczak now agreed, that only with Solidarity's full participation was there a chance of turning Poland's economy around.

The roundtable deal

If it is possible to pinpoint the first tremors of Poland's revolution, they were certainly felt during the roundtable meetings between the government and Solidarity in February and March 1989. (In truth, most of the roundtable meetings were held at many different rectangular tables, each with really just two sides, Communist authorities on one side and the Solidarity-opposition on the other.) Walesa attended the first meeting and then had to race around the country trying to extinguish an ever-expanding number of wildcat strikes. During the two months of negotiations, the Polish people held their breath. According to one student, "It was hard to accept the fact that the government was postured to listen—not lecture. I wasn't sure it was a sincere position for them to take."

It is hard to imagine a more dramatic situation, as former prisoners negotiated face to face with their former jailers and tormentors. During the negotiations, extraordinary stories circulated around the country. One concerned Zbigniew Bujak, Solidarity's legendary Warsaw leader, who for more than four years evaded arrest after the imposition of martial law. Apparently, Bujak had some close calls: Once he literally ran out of his sheepskin coat as he was being nabbed by security agents, leaving them holding nothing but the coat. During the talks, the story goes, Bujak found himself negotiating with General Kiszczak, the man who had even-

The first roundtable meeting between Poland's Communist government and Solidarity leaders, February 6, 1989. During two months of negotiations, Poland took large steps toward pluralism and democracy. (CAF/Warszawa)

tually succeeded in jailing him. "By the way," the General told Bujak at the roundtable, "I have your coat in my office. You're welcome to come by and pick it up whenever you like."

The results of the roundtable meetings changed the course of Poland's history—and the history of Eastern Europe. A remarkable but risky deal was born. It was a compromise deal, but an open-ended compromise. Announced on April 5, the following were the most impressive points:

> The restoration of Solidarity, the trade union that was formed in 1980 and then banned after martial law was imposed in 1981. Also, the promise of legalization for an independent students' union.
>
> Elections on June 4, 1989, for a two-house Parliament, in which free competition would be permitted for 35 percent of the 460 seats in the existing lower house, the Sejm.
>
> The restoration of the upper house, or Senate, which was disbanded after World War II. It would have 100 members, who would be chosen in completely free elections. The upper house would be able to veto legislation of the lower house.
>
> The establishment of the post of president of the republic; the holder would be elected by the two houses of Parliament for a six-year term. The president would have broad powers to dissolve Parliament and to veto laws passed by the lower house. The lower house could overturn vetoes by a two-thirds vote.
>
> Vast changes in the structure of the economy, including the installment of a wage-indexing plan, by which workers and re- tired people would receive compensation covering up to 80 percent of any increase in the cost of living.

For Solidarity, it was a staggering moment of triumph. Walesa's name was chanted in the streets. In an official statement, Walesa said, "I have to emphasize that for the first time we have talked to each other using the force of arguments, and not arguments of force. It bids well for the future, I believe. The roundtable talks can become the beginning of the road for democracy and a free Poland." The Polish people wanted nothing less. Walesa continued,

"Either we will be able to build Poland as a nation in a peaceful way, independent, sovereign and safe, with equal alliances, or we will sink in the chaos of demagogy, which could result in a civil war in which there will be no victors."

The most ambitious gain, in addition to the relegalization of the union, was the announcement that the Communists would give up 35 percent of the 460 seats in the lower house. It really meant that the Communists would hold only 38 percent of the lower house—the smallest percentage since World War II. The remainder of the seats would fall to small parties that, until now, had collaborated with the Communists in a ruling coalition. Perhaps the most startling concession, however, was the government's agreement to restore Poland's upper house of Parliament with free and open elections.

The Communist authorities left the talks slightly dazed. They had, however, managed to secure a guaranteed majority in the Sejm. They also got Solidarity's agreement to an early election in June, thus giving the opposition virtually no time to organize a campaign starting from less than scratch. In addition, the constitution would include the powerful office of president, which was expected to go to General Jaruzelski.

It is important to remember that all of these maneuvers took place against the background of rising economic chaos. A government report published in January 1989 confirmed that the per capita gross national product was still 13 percent lower than it had been ten years before and that inflation exceeded 60 percent. The economic crisis gave the opposition an advantage—the government needed popular support to give its reforms a chance. Just as urgently, Solidarity feared a bloody explosion that it could not control.

Only weeks after the deal was made, there was a critical division among the Communist leadership. When hard-line Party officials attempted to derail the agreement with Solidarity, Jaruzelski threatened to resign, along with other key leaders including Prime Minister Rakowski, General Kiszczak, and Defense Minister Florian Siwicki. The deal with Solidarity nearly collapsed. But the disastrous state of the Polish economy left the Party no more promising alternative.

Greater opportunities

A week after the conclusion of the roundtable talks, *Tygodnik Mazowsze* (*Mazowsze Weekly*), Warsaw's bold underground weekly, published its last issue. Produced for more than seven years with astonishing regularity, *Tygodnik* was distributing as many as eighty thousand copies a week by the end of the run. In its last issue, the staff members finally revealed their real names. There was no longer much danger of arrest. They also announced that within a few weeks they would reassemble under the banner of *Gazeta Wyborcza* (*The Election News*), the Eastern bloc's first legal opposition daily since the days of Solidarity, with a projected circulation in excess of five hundred thousand. Permission to publish such a daily had been another of the conditions squeezed from the Party at the roundtable talks.

The final statement of the *Tygodnik* staff captured the mood of the moment: "We are all aware of the fact that the present political situation is precarious and uncertain, that the official declarations are not trustworthy, and that we run a great risk of losing all we have and getting nothing in return. Still, this is a new situation: Solidarity is becoming a legal union; the elections are imminent—and, though they are undemocratic, we can win or lose them. Therefore, in such a moment to run away from risk and play for time would mean giving up these new, much *greater opportunities* to work on behalf of the ideals for which we have been struggling for years—the ideals of Solidarity."

June 4 elections

Working against tremendous odds, Solidarity mounted an effective, if somewhat confusing, campaign. The union staged impressive rallies in every district of the country. Still, most observers were, at best, hopeful about the election's outcome. Early election morning, Warsaw blossomed with one last flowering of Solidarity posters: a photograph of Gary Cooper, in full sheriff's regalia (though minus the gun, which had been whited out of the image), striding toward the viewer, the union's red logo emblazoned on the horizon behind

The *Gazeta Wyborcza* (*The Election News*), the Soviet bloc's first legal opposition daily. Its publication marked the emergence of a free press in Eastern Europe. (CAF/ Warszawa)

him, with the simple caption "HIGH NOON." (The Communist party's primary slogan was, "With us, you're safer.")

That day, as the Chinese army shot at demonstrators calling for more democracy in Tiananmen Square in Beijing, Poles were lining up to vote in the freest elections ever held under Communist rule. The news of the election returns was almost drowned out— even in *Gazeta Wyborcza's* own coverage—by the tragic developments in Tiananmen Square. The Poles observed the Chinese events with horror, seeing in them part of their own, earlier bloody uprisings.

Solidarity was overwhelmingly victorious, winning 260 of the 261 seats it was contesting. In a stunning defeat, the ruling Communist party failed to win even one of the seats for which there was a competitive race. The Communists even lost races where they ran unopposed. Unopposed candidates were required to pick up at least 50 percent of the votes cast. Because they failed to get 50 percent, their seats were declared vacant. In fact, the vast majority of voters delighted in crossing out the Communist candidates' names, one at a time. Voters in most of the 108 districts gave the Communists dismal returns, ranging from 25 percent to as little as 5 percent or less. Virtually all of the regime's 35 unopposed candidates—including Rakowski, Kiszczak, and Siwicki—lost their elections.

The Solidarity that emerged triumphant in June 1989, after a long and bitter struggle, was not the same Solidarity that had captured the imagination of the world in 1980. At that time, Solidarity was a gleaming opposition movement that boasted more than ten million members and represented the hopes of the majority of the Polish people. Almost a decade later, it was a different organization. It lacked its former breadth of support and unity of purpose. Poles with more radical views regarded Walesa and other leaders of the movement as collaborators or traitors for cooperating with the Communist regime. Some Poles criticized as undemocratic the methods by which Solidarity candidates were selected for the June elections. In several parts of the country, groups unaffiliated with Solidarity sprang up in response to local problems.

If the 1989 election proved nothing else, it exposed the failure of the Communist party to win and hold the support of the people it had ruled for more than 40 years. The outcome was less of a triumph for Solidarity than a near-total rejection of communism.

Solidarity's first day in Parliament

Solidarity, vilified and outlawed for eight years, entered the lower house of Parliament jubilantly on July 4, 1989. It was the first freely elected opposition party to do so in a communist country. Solidarity had grown from a union of workers into a huge political force. As the assembly opened, Walesa sat in the place of honor of Poland's newest institution—the opposition front bench. On the Communist front sat Jaruzelski, the man who imposed martial law to crush the movement in 1981.

Later in the day, when the newly created Senate gathered for the first time, Jaruzelski and Walesa sat together in the front row as guests of honor, smiling and chatting for a moment as the proceedings began. The Senate offered no Communist permanent bench to accommodate Jaruzelski, because Solidarity swept 99 of the 100 seats (losing one to an independent).

Hundreds of people watched from the visitors' gallery. Among them, off to one side, were Rakowski, Kiszczak, Siwicki, and many other members of the Politburo, the Communist party's policy-making and executive committee. The voters had denied them the right to sit as elected officials in this body of government. The losers sat quietly, talking softly among one another and, according to one reporter, "unsmilingly enduring the cameras that were constantly trained on them from the press box." They looked down at those whom until recently their Party and government had jailed as dissidents.

Creating a new government

A great deal of political jockeying occurred before the emergence of a Solidarity-led government in September. In July, the issue was the election of the nation's president. According to the Polish constitution, the person in this powerful office was to be elected by the members of both houses of Parliament. On July 19, Jaruzelski was elected by a vote of 270 to 267. After his election to the presidency, Jaruzelski fulfilled an earlier pledge by resigning as the head of the Communist party. Rakowski, the defeated prime minister, was chosen as the Party's new leader, by a vote of 171 to 41 in the Party's Central Committee.

On August 2, the Communists successfully pushed through Parliament the Party's nominee for prime minister. Czeslaw Kiszczak was elected with a margin of 26 votes after regaining the support of the Peasant party, a long-time ally of the Communist party, which had been promised additional seats in the Council of Ministers. Over the next few weeks, Kiszczak struggled to form a grand coalition—a government of national unity. He approached some of the top Solidarity leaders and urged them to accept jobs in various ministries. One Solidarity leader dismissed Kiszczak's proposals, saying that Kiszczak was offering Solidarity only the "Ministry of Debts, the Ministry of Wretched Housing, and the Ministry of Abysmal Labor."

As the Communists struggled to build a coalition, it grew more and more apparent that they were in trouble. They would not be able to rule on their own. The small, once-obedient parties that collaborated with the Communists for so long now found it more advantageous to cut deals with Solidarity. This deprived the Communist party of its guaranteed majority of seats in the lower house.

Solidarity's leaders invited the Peasant party and the Democratic party, another Communist ally, to join them in a small, "interesting kind of coalition." Lech Walesa added, "Forget about the Grand Coalition; it's time to form a little coalition."

Through "back-door" negotiations, Walesa managed to dislodge entire delegations of both puppet parties from their decades-long collaboration with the Communists. Many Solidarity officials in Parliament were appalled. "How can we form a government with hypocrites?" one leader asked. "I would rather work beside the Communists." But the smallest parties, too, could see the developing trend. Looking four years ahead, they realized they had better assert their independence if they wanted to hold on to any power at all. Furthermore, Walesa offered them senior posts in the new government.

On August 14, under increasing Soviet pressure for an end to Poland's government crisis, Prime Minister Kiszczak announced that he would step down. He added that it would be "prudent for the nation to choose a prime minister traditionally allied with the Communist party." Three days later, Walesa, along with top leaders from the Peasant and Democratic parties, presented to President Jaruzelski the candidacy of Tadeusz Mazowiecki. A prominent Catholic editor and lawyer with extensive political experience, Mazowiecki had played a major role in the creation of Solidarity in 1980. He had also worked as editor-in-chief of *Tygodnik Solidarnosc* (*Solidarity Weekly*), the Eastern bloc's fully independent weekly.

Mazowiecki was elected prime minister on August 24. For the first time since 1948, Poland had a non-Communist leader heading its government. But the huge task the new prime minister faced, that of reviving an exhausted and inefficient economy, cast a shadow of uncertainty over his chances of success.

Tadeusz Mazowiecki

The election of the new prime minister was a perfect example of the alliance between workers and intellectuals that made Solidarity unique. The alliance was cemented in 1980 when Mazowiecki wrote an appeal, signed by 64 scholars, in support of the Gdansk shipyard workers. The document read: "In this struggle, the place of the entire intelligentsia is on their side. That is the Polish tradition, and that is the imperative of the hour." On behalf of the signers, Mazowiecki delivered the document to Walesa, who thanked him warmly. "But what we need are not petitions," Walesa told him. "What we need are experts, someone like you, to talk to the government on our behalf. Please give us your help." Mazowiecki agreed to stay on in Gdansk as advisor to Solidarity, and after the union was outlawed, he helped guide its underground activities. The new prime minister was not schooled in economics or administration. But with the triumph of Solidarity, he found himself with the task of somehow putting Poland on the road to economic recovery.

When Mazowiecki returned to Gdansk as prime minister nine years later, he admitted that "Poland needed bread more than it needed a prime minister." He told the crowds of well-wishers, "Today, when we open this historic chapter, we must reject a feeling of hopelessness. It must be rejected because no one can do anything without believing that it can be done."

Building a market economy

Mazowiecki's government was approved by Parliament on September 12, 1989. The initial 23-member cabinet had 11 seats for Solidarity, including most of the key economic ministries, and 4 seats for the Communists, including the ministries of Foreign Trade, Defense, Transportation, and the Interior. The 7 additional seats were occupied by the Peasant and Democratic parties. The Ministry of Foreign Affairs was headed by a pro-Solidarity independent.

It was no coincidence that Solidarity held the seats that would deal with economic problems. The economic crisis was the greatest challenge facing the new Mazowiecki government. What was wrong with the economy? There is a Polish saying, popular throughout Eastern Europe under communism, that underscored the problem: "There is no unemployment, but no one works. No one works, but the plan is always fulfilled. The plan is fulfilled, but there is nothing to buy." One housewife complained, "The Polish economy is so unsound that you can't buy what you want, you have to buy what's available. You can't buy the cheaper product, because it's not there. It's at the point where an average Polish worker makes in a month what a Western worker makes in an hour, and yet he often can't economize, because the cheaper product is not available."

These stories combined with the hard statistics filled the new leaders with terror. For the second year in a row, the availability of food products was far below the average for 1983 to 1986. During the summer of 1989, the Finance Ministry warned that the domestic market was in danger of collapse; many shops were already completely bare of food. The inflation rate exceeded 150 percent and was soaring. Industrial production was falling. Although there was a positive trend in the country's foreign-trade balance in 1988, the staggering foreign debt—39 billion dollars to the West and 6 billion rubles to the Soviet Union—continued to be a burden. Interest payments alone totaled nearly 4 billion dollars a year.

Would the new government be able to inspire enough confidence from the Polish people—who had seen economic plans come and go with few, if any, results—to introduce reforms? Economists spoke of the need for a "shock plan." The first practical step toward this plan came on September 15, when price controls were removed from food products. When the shock program went into effect, it provided a rude awakening. Almost overnight, communism's empty shelves and endless lines vanished. Butcher shops were filled with sausages and hams, television stores with televisions, gas stations with gas. A nervous mixture of fear and exhilaration swept through the population. The catch was that nobody could afford to buy the available goods. Prices had soared. The lifting of food price controls was helping to feed inflation. After a few weeks, prices began to fall a little and inflation cooled.

One of the April roundtable agreements called for the economy to be based on market principles. In other words, Poland wanted to return to capitalism. Many Poles shook their heads and, half smiling, wondered what, if anything, was achieved by the decades of communism. A common joke ran, "What is communism? It is the longest road from capitalism to capitalism."

In October, the Mazowiecki government unveiled details of a preliminary plan to rapidly convert Poland to a market economy. During the first phase, the government would move quickly to reduce state ownership of property, reform the state budget and the banking system, and break up monopolies in an attempt to create competition and make state enterprises more efficient. Realizing bankruptcy and unemployment would result in some cases from these changes, the government attempted to soften their effect by instituting unemployment benefits and other social security measures. In mid-October, Parliament moved to offset the burden of inflation by compensating workers for about 80 percent of increases in the prices of food and manufactured goods.

There was a general understanding when Mazowiecki took office that things would get worse before they got better. But as the months passed, the determination with which many people initially met sacrifice began to slowly erode. Many people were suddenly complaining and acting as if the economic crisis was started by Solidarity. A prominent newspaper journalist counseled his readers: "Be patient, will you? We have worked so hard to install a government we trust. Tell the political groups to calm down and that they threaten to ruin everything we have built. They threaten to destabilize the crucial political balance and to weaken the emerging democracy. Mazowiecki's government should be given time to carry out its program in peace."

Turning inside out

By January 1990, it was clear that the economic plan was doing what it was supposed to. Inflation had fallen from the 78 percent monthly rate in December 1989 to just over 4 percent. But the structure of the Polish economy had not yet changed. Apart from the appearance of huge numbers of private street vendors crowding the city sidewalks selling meat, butter, cheese, and bread, the democratic government had not been able to dislodge itself from the old communist monopolies.

One of the master plans of the Communist government in Poland had been to gain control of the entire economic life of the country. This way, the government claimed, every citizen could be assured an equal piece of the pie, as well as the same opportunities and the same financial stability. This control included owning every factory and every farm. It meant that all shops, hotels, restaurants, cafes, bookstores, publishing firms, and cinemas would be owned and operated by the Communist government. To a large extent, the four decades of Communist regimes succeeded in gaining ownership of such industries. Unfortunately, the system failed to provide people with even their most basic needs.

During his first year as prime minister, Mazowiecki struggled to "turn the economic structures inside out." How could they return the government enterprises back to private ownership? Ac-

For many Poles, the Mazowiecki government did not act
quickly enough to remove Soviet troops from Polish soil.
These students have just finished hanging anti-Soviet posters
during a demonstration near the city of Lublin. The poster at
left shows a Soviet soldier saying, "Mazowiecki, send me
home!" (CAF/Warszawa)

cording to most news reports, privatization was stalled for political
reasons. The government simply could not get Parliament to agree.
To begin with, there was the question of who to sell the state
businesses to. The Ministry of Finance wanted to take bids from
the first paying customers—with few questions asked. Solidarity
officials in Parliament insisted that workers be given preferential
access to the shares in their factory.

The paradoxical truth was that the current management—from
the ranks of Communist party membership—were generally better
qualified to become the country's new industrial entrepreneurs.
Eager not to imitate the purges of its Communist predecessors,
the Mazowiecki government was slow to replace these thousands
of managers and civil servants. Thus, the Polish Communists
shrewdly converted their managerial posts in state enterprises into
ownership shares. The remarkable thing about this strategy was its

nerve. Is it right that the people who impoverished and brutalized their nation claim a major role in its future?

The ecological crisis

Even if the Solidarity government does manage to push through a transition to a free market economy, control unemployment, and restore private ownership, there remain longer-term challenges. During the 1980s, Poland faced three crises: a political crisis, an economic crisis, and an ecological crisis. Of the three, the political crisis was the "easiest" to solve. It was quickly addressed by the election of Mazowiecki in August 1989. The economic crisis continues, as the government struggles to pass new laws that will encourage a market economy. The ecological crisis, however, may be the toughest of the three. The average life expectancy in Poland is about ten years less than that of the rest of Europe. This is a statistic most doctors blame squarely on the country's unhealthy environment.

Poland and many other Eastern European countries face some of the greatest ecological devastation on the planet. The Communist leaders simply had no interest in controlling the reckless effects of their industrial development. The city of Krakow, for example, once called "the pearl of all European cities," is gasping for air. Although it survived Nazi occupation, it is not clear how it will be salvaged from the years of Communist mismanagement. Since the early 1950s, the Lenin Steelworks (the largest in Europe) discharged unknown quantities of yellow, brown, and red gases into the skies near Krakow. As a result, the region's gentle rains have literally eaten away the faces, hands, and other details of the countless medieval statues throughout the city.

Another sad example is the Vistula River, Poland's chief waterway. It winds lazily through the flat lowlands of the country and through many of its major cities. For most of its length, it is a toxic sewer. In Gdansk Harbor, where the Vistula River empties into the Baltic Sea, the flounder, eel, and herring have either left or died off. Fish caught in the harbor stink so badly when cooked that they are called "diesel fish."

Today, Poland faces stark choices over its ecology crisis. Now that Poland has opened its doors to foreign investment, many competing enterprises threaten to ruin the already ravaged environment. Given a choice between dumping wastes on the way to greater profits or initiating strict environmental regulations, it is hard to imagine that the government would endanger economic growth. As one journalist asked, "Will local governments, given their small, overextended budgets, be more likely to invest in soup kitchens for the unemployed or in sewage treatment plants?" Even during the fall of 1989, Poland started to receive all sorts of proposals for foreign joint ventures. Many proposed the construction of huge hotels and fancy resorts. Naturally, the foreign entrepreneurs focused on the most beautiful and unspoiled districts of the country. As one official said, "Poland is in desperate need of investment, so it cannot afford to be choosy."

Lech Walesa campaigning for the presidency in Fall 1990.
(CAF/Warszawa)

Solidarity in power

After 45 years of Communist rule, the Polish economy is in worse shape than ever before. Many of the economic defects of the old Communist government are still in place, while the disadvantages of a market economy—unemployment and bankruptcies—are already evident. Government and World Bank projections predict unemployment will rise to two million in 1991—more than ten percent of the population. The Solidarity-led Parliament is understandably reluctant to back measures that will throw its supporters out of jobs. The Communists, slimmed down from two million to 70,000 members and repackaged as the Social Democratic party, are now articulate advocates of the new democratic system. They do not have a very high profile, however.

More than a year after the collapse of communism in Poland, the country is still building its democracy. Many Poles are beginning to realize that the years under the totalitarian leadership of the Communist party created a society in which democracy is not easily adapted. "It is hard work," one Parliament member said. "It's easier to break out of prison than to know what to do once you're out," said another member. Last year, the extreme unpopularity of the country's former rulers was an obvious spur to political activity. Volunteers sprang out of the woodwork. Today, now that they have overthrown the Communists, many Poles regard running for public office and getting involved with dread. The current public apathy—whether from the exhaustion of making ends meet, dissatisfaction with the recent government, or simply not understanding the process of democracy—is dangerous.

Nonetheless, Poland has ended the period when national politics could be divided between the Solidarity movement and the Communist party. That is a remarkable achievement. Today, it is a division between people who want things to happen quickly and those who want things to happen slowly. The people who want things to happen quickly are more numerous. Voting against Mazowiecki's careful and slow strategy of reform, Lech Walesa was elected President on December 9, 1990. He won 75 percent of the vote.

Adam Michnik is one of the great heroes of Poland's revolution.

He endured countless arrests, detentions, interrogations, searches, beatings, and spent more than six years in Communist prisons. Today, he serves in Poland's Parliament. Michnik has written that the present period of transition from dictatorship to democracy requires a compromise among the main political forces. *"There must be a pact for democracy,"* he wrote. He warned that the breaking of this pact will betray the revolution, make each step a hardship, and will introduce chaos. "And chaos cannot be reformed. Chaos will return us to dictatorship."

2 HUNGARY

The Quiet Revolution

Hungarian border guards dismantling the Iron Curtain that divided Europe for four decades. (Reuters/Bettmann Archives)

A Chronology of Events in Hungary

February 1946	Hungary is declared a republic after the abolition of the monarchy.
August 1947	Elections give the Communist-dominated leftist block 46 percent of the vote.
October/ November 1956	Imre Nagy becomes prime minister; more than twenty thousand people are killed in two waves of Soviet invasions.
November 1956	Nagy is replaced by Janos Kadar.
February 11, 1989	The government approves the creation of independent parties.
March 1989	More than 75 thousand march in Budapest calling for the withdrawal of Soviet troops and free elections.
May 2, 1989	Hungary begins dismantling its portion of the iron curtain along its border with Austria.
May 8, 1989	Janos Kadar is replaced by Karoly Grosz as general secretary.
June 16, 1989	Imre Nagy is reburied in a huge anti-Communist rally.
September 10, 1989	Border with Austria is opened to East Germans wishing to leave.

October 7, 1989	The Communist party dissolves itself and becomes the Socialist party.
October 23, 1989	Hungary declares itself "independent and legal."
March 25, 1990	Jozsef Antall of the Hungarian Democratic Forum is elected prime minister.

IN MOST EASTERN EUROPEAN CAPITALS in 1989, May Day (the traditional day celebrating communism in Communist countries) was staged with all the usual festivities: slogans, red banners, military marching bands, Communist girl scouts, tanks, and missiles. But May Day was a big flop that year for the Communists of Budapest; only a few thousand people turned out for the annual festivities. On the other side of town, however, a rally called by Hungary's Communist opposition attracted more than one hundred thousand people. The next day, as workers were cleaning up the remains of the rally, Hungarian guards along the Hungarian-Austrian border received orders from Budapest to snip away hundreds of yards of barbed wire along the so-called iron curtain. "Breaching the iron curtain was meant to attract some support for the Party," wrote one journalist. Instead, "it had the same effect as piercing a small hole in the hull of a large ship in the middle of a stormy sea."

Hungary's whirlwind

Hungary is not like the rest of Eastern Europe. The Hungarian Revolution of 1989 was spearheaded not by opposition leaders or crowds of protesters, but by reform-minded Communists. Of them, Imre Pozsgay was the most influential. He was an original thinker who pushed for change when it was risky to do so. Leading a revolution from top down, Pozsgay became the country's most popular politician. As early as 1987, Pozsgay was arguing that a new Hungary should be modeled on the democracies of Western

Europe. In the remarkable fall of 1989, Pozsgay said, "It's time for Communism to disappear. Now we must create a constitutional state." As that process began, Pozsgay was the front-runner for president in Hungary's first free elections since World War II. By late 1989, censorship was abolished and a free press emerged. A new stock market heralded the beginning of free enterprise. The Communist party received a face-lift. Even the red stars on public buildings were removed. In fact, the 90-foot statue of Lenin next to the biggest square in Budapest was carted away. Officially, it was removed for renovation; a few months later, a committee started by the mayor of Budapest decided that, for "aesthetic" reasons, it would be kept in storage permanently. After more than 40 years of Soviet-style communism, Hungary said goodbye to Lenin.

The insurrection of 1956

Many Eastern Europeans thought Stalin's death in 1953 would signal immediate change. The new Soviet leader, Nikita Khrushchev, denounced the brutality of the Stalin regime. He even suggested that "different roads to socialism" were possible. Disappointment mounted in Hungary, however, as repression by Soviet leaders continued even after Stalin's death. Of the ten million people who lived in Hungary in early 1954, more than 640,000 were imprisoned. Hungarians demanded that the Party relax its controls and "open doors to the West." Since the occupation of Hungary by Stalin's troops in World War II, the borders had been tightly sealed. People could not even visit former Hungarian villages that had been absorbed by neighboring Romania or Czechoslovakia. Families were separated.

In October 1956, only a few days after news of Poland's uprising reached Hungary, huge demonstrations of sympathy for the Poles occurred in Budapest. Someone suggested marching on to Parliament. By the time the demonstrators reached that grand building along the Danube River, they numbered hundreds of thousands. According to one spectator, "Calls went out for Imre Nagy, the most reform-minded Communist leader. Part of the crowd toppled the huge statue of Stalin. After the secret police fired on the crowd, soldiers joined the demonstrators and distributed arms."

Desperate to prevent more unrest, the Communist party named Nagy prime minister. Pushed by enthusiastic crowds, the new leader promised to disband the secret police. He undertook a brave but dangerous policy of changing Hungary's relationship with the Soviet Union. "From the youngest child to the oldest man," Nagy said, "no one wants communism. We have had enough of it forever." Nagy called for the removal of Soviet troops and the ultimate neutralization of Hungary. He even went so far as to call for the withdrawal of Hungary from the Warsaw Pact.

These policies were completely unacceptable to the Soviet Union. In early November, an infuriated Khrushchev dispatched two hundred thousand troops to Hungary backed with massive units of tanks and artillery. Hungarian suicide squads hurled Molotov cocktails, paving stones, even sticks at the invaders. Sniper fire rained down from the top floors of the buildings in the city center. Soviet tanks responded by destroying entire buildings. Soldiers used automatic gunfire to cut down the patriots.

In a matter of weeks, the insurrection of 1956 was over. More than twenty thousand people had been killed. Some two hundred thousand people had either escaped into the West or were soon pushed out of their homeland by the Soviets. Before their withdrawal, the Soviets set up a "puppet" government, controlled by the Soviets and headed by the hard-line Communist Janos Kadar.

The Butcher of Budapest

Only days before the Soviet invasion, Janos Kadar had praised the rebels for their "glorious uprising," and voted with Imre Nagy in favor of a multi-party democracy and Hungarian neutrality. When the Soviets offered him the job of returning Hungary to "socialism," he quickly accepted the task. Now a Soviet armored car delivered him to Parliament, where he declared the insurrection a "counterrevolution." Show trials and executions followed. Hungarians nicknamed Kadar "the Butcher of Budapest."

Kadar had the difficult job of making the rebellious Hungarians

During the 1956 Soviet invasion of Hungary, a Soviet tank
trains its guns on a shell-shattered residence in Budapest.
(Reuters/Bettmann Archives)

loyal to Moscow. Of course, he never succeeded. But by a series
of ruthless measures, Kadar extinguished the hopes of his people.
Haunted by the agony of the uprising, Hungarians remained pas-

sive. "After 1956, people asked for nothing and received nothing," one Hungarian has written. "We didn't want to treat the government like a government, so we ignored it. How could we ask for change? Consider what happened to us the last time we asked for change."

The final blow to their revolutionary spirit was the execution of Imre Nagy in 1958. The brutal, open show of force by Moscow in Budapest and Hungary's subsequent regime of terror destroyed illusions about the benevolence of Stalin's successors.

Kadar's puppet government ruled Hungary for 31 years. In all that time, he refused to discuss the events of 1956. He and his government simply pretended that nothing had happened. The Party never admitted any wrongdoing and never accepted responsibility for the bloodshed. In 1985, a Party leader tried to explain: "We have spoken little of the lessons of 1956 because we wanted to clear away the waste, we wanted to heal the wounds, we wanted to eliminate from people's lives the suspicion, the mistrust, the constant feeling of political danger." By 1985, talking about the "lessons of 1956" was not enough for most Hungarians. They certainly did not want to be lectured about 1956 by the government that killed their hero.

Goulash communism

Some changes occurred in the mid-1960s as Kadar's government began to shuffle its feet. Kadar wanted to refashion his image among the people. He received permission from the Soviet Union to experiment with the Hungarian economy. Without challenging Moscow, he installed a series of market-oriented economic reforms and relaxed the political atmosphere. As long as Hungarians did not openly dissent, they enjoyed significant personal freedom.

This clever compromise became known as "goulash communism." The economic reforms freed the country from many of the stifling restrictions built into other Soviet-type economies. For example, Kadar encouraged a limited amount of private enterprise. Hungarians embraced this flawed bargain throughout the 1970s and 1980s. It was better to have stores filled with tempting goods, even without the money to buy them, than to have empty stores and lots of useless money. Elegant cafes, colorful, well-stocked shops, and grand restaurants lined the streets of Budapest. Even Western tourists were surprised by the "capitalist" facade. Underneath, however, Hungary was crumbling.

The reburial of Imre Nagy

In 1989, 31 years after he was hanged and his body thrown into a prison grave, Imre Nagy was given a solemn funeral on Budapest's largest square, followed by a hero's burial. Only a year before, when the opposition held a small demonstration to mark the 30th anniversary of Nagy's murder, the police were brought in to disperse it. The Party had warned the "democratic opposition" not to go through with their plans. Using strong language, the Party threatened to use "administrative measures" to suppress "enemy and opposition" demonstrations. It was an unfortunate choice of words. Under Hungary's Stalinist government in the early 1950s, "administrative measures" were synonymous with mass arrests, show trials, and torture. In fact, a small demonstration did take place, and the police used truncheons and tear gas against the participants. Twelve months later, in June 1989, those same police assisted in preparing an extraordinary public, ceremonial reburial of the leader of the 1956 insurrection and those executed with him in June 1958.

On Heroes' Square, the great neoclassical columns were draped in black. From the colonnades hung huge green, white, and red national flags. Each flag had the circle cut out of its center, as the insurgents had cut out the hammer and sickle, the symbol of communism, in 1956. Six coffins lay on the steps of the temple-like Gallery of Art. Five of the coffins represented Imre Nagy and his closest associates. The sixth coffin was symbolic of the Unknown Insurgent.

Funeral music sounded from the loudspeakers, as the people lined up under the burning sun to lay flowers in tribute to their martyrs. First, and most movingly, came two ordinary people quietly placing one or two carnations. Then came the official dele-

The reburial of Imre Nagy, hero of the 1956 insurrection,
changed the course of Hungarian history. The ceremony
galvanized the Hungarians' desire for freedom from
Communism. (AP/Wide World Photos)

gations with large, formal wreaths: local councils, clergy, Western
diplomats, a delegation from Warsaw for Polish-Hungarian Solidarity. There were a few reformist Hungarian party politicians,
formally representing the government and the Parliament. There
were, however, no delegations to formally represent the Hungarian
Communist party. There were none present from the Soviet Union
either.

The speeches were even more remarkable. "Will freedom for
Hungary grow from the blood of these heroes?" asked the old man
who was the head of the Budapest Workers' Councils in 1956.
"There are some obstacles," he said. The first obstacle was the
presence of Soviet troops on Hungarian soil. The second obstacle
was the Communist party, clinging to power. The third obstacle
was the fragmentation of social forces.

The last speaker was a student. "If we can trust our souls and strength," he said, "we can put an end to the communist dictatorship; if we are determined enough we can force the Party to submit itself to free elections; and if we do not lose sight of the ideals of 1956, then we will be able to elect a government that will start immediate negotiations about the swift withdrawal of Russian troops." The subdued crowd, perhaps two hundred thousand strong, was finally roused to fierce applause. Everything was broadcast live on national television.

Later the same day, a small group traveled to the remote corner of the cemetery where, sometime after the execution, the remains of Nagy and his associates were cast into a common grave. For many years, Party officials used the burial site as a garbage dump. But now the ground was prepared for a decent burial. They even laid a new road to the site and lined it with a guard of honor.

One name not mentioned in any of the speeches, but in everyone's thoughts, was Janos Kadar. Kadar was remembered not as the leader of Hungary from 1956 to 1988, but as the traitor who took over from Nagy on "the back of Soviet tanks." In everyone's mind, Kadar was responsible for the murder of Imre Nagy. He had signed the death sentence. Where was Kadar on this hot, memorable day in June 1989? Was he at home watching the funeral on television? According to one spectator, "This is not the funeral of Imre Nagy. It is the resurrection of Imre Nagy, and the funeral of Janos Kadar."

Three weeks after the reburial of Nagy, Kadar died. On the same day, the Hungarian Supreme Court finalized the decision to restore the honor of the leaders of the 1956 insurrection.

How things changed

Why did this astonishing reburial take place? Why did the Communist party permit it? Where did the Hungarian people get their nerve? Unfortunately, these are hard questions to answer. "The origins of the new Hungarian Revolution," one journalist has written, "are rooted in many layers of questions."

The first turning point came in January 1988 when the editors of an important Hungarian Communist journal asked a very surprising question: "To what extent is the Party willing to share power? And who actually sets the limits?" Hungary's Communist party claimed to be entering a period of "renewal." Remembering Tocqueville's warning, the Party was careful not to use the word "reform."

In May 1988, Kadar's long rule ended abruptly when a Party conference voted to replace him with Karoly Grosz. Within a year, Kadar was expelled from the Party's Central Committee as well as from his last, purely ceremonial post as president of the Party. Kadar soon drifted into the darker shadows of Hungarian history.

The pace of "renewal" in Hungary accelerated dramatically after Kadar's removal from office. Then, in June 1989, the Central Committee demoted Grosz and established a "collective quartet of leadership." Under Grosz's chairmanship, the quartet promised to continue the "spirit of reform." Almost immediately, they set out to distance the Communist party from its Stalinist and Kadarist past. They called for more "social tolerance" and started a campaign to polish the Party's tarnished image.

Was Hungary like Poland?

As Hungary's Communist government was struggling to "renew" itself, major changes were unfolding in Communist Poland. As one observer of the Eastern European situation has written, "It was a springtime for two nations. Future historians will have to explain how Poland and Hungary, starting from such different circumstances at the beginning of the 1980s, came to such relatively similar positions at the end of the decade."

The basic elements were the same in Poland and Hungary. Both governments were police-party states, able to rule because they could call upon enormous military resources. They also shared a lack of legitimacy. As far as opposition movements were concerned, both Poland and Hungary had articulate anti-Communists. But Poland's anti-Communists were world famous, thanks to the Solidarity era. Moreover, the Poles had built up a huge worker-intellectual-farmer-based opposition, compared with the intelligentsia-based opposition in Hungary. Nonetheless, the opposition in both countries wanted the same thing: to turn their countries into what they called "normal" countries. When they said "normal," they meant Western European, liberal, democratic, with a market economy, a freely elected parliament, and an independent judicial system.

Interestingly, the roundtable deal that Solidarity made with the Communist authorities in Poland was held up as a positive example by Hungary's Party officials. The opposition, however, thought it was a negative example. "With all due respect to the Poles," one opposition leader said, "we can do it faster." They certainly knew what they wanted. The Poles were "rather afraid to come out and say it." But they did not hesitate, when the opportunity came, to say it eloquently. The Hungarians followed their lead. During the summer of 1989, they presented some of their demands to the Communist party: "We want free elections, with no handicaps, no quotas, no new upper house. After free elections, the one sovereign and freely elected parliament must form the new government and create a new constitution."

Faced with such demands, the Hungarian leadership retreated more quickly than the Polish leadership had. In fact, they retreated faster in front of a smaller, less powerful, opposition movement. Why? Part of the answer, according to one Hungarian, was "they couldn't think of any reason not to." Heavily influenced by contact with the West, Hungarian Party officials really could not think of any reason why they should *not* give up power. (Budapest is only about 100 miles from Vienna, but thousands of miles from Moscow.) A second reason was the indecision of the Party leader, Karoly Grosz. Though he was hailed as a tough and decisive leader when he took over from Janos Kadar in 1988, he turned out to be surprisingly weak and indecisive.

A third reason was that the Hungarian Party was already in the process of "renewal" (reform), unlike the Polish Communists. The signs of disarray in the Party were unmistakable. They had to reform because their numbers were shrinking. Asked about his Party membership, a well-known scholar said, "I am leaving the Party because I don't want to be taken for an opportunist." Although the size of the Party apparatus was also getting smaller, it became very difficult to fill Party vacancies. They hoped that reform would attract new members.

The fourth reason may be the most significant. The Party could not agree on how to proceed. A senior official said it clearly in February 1989: "There are now three parties in one. There is the one made up of social reformers led by Imre Pozsgay. There are the moderate pragmatic socialists led by Prime Minister Nemeth, and there are the true old-fashioned Communists who keep putting their hopes on Karoly Grosz."

In fact, a struggle for power was taking place at the top of the Party. Through the early part of 1989, Imre Pozsgay continually forced the pace of the Party's retreat. He believed that "far-reaching reforms would improve the credibility of the Party among the people." As early as January 1989, Pozsgay convinced the Party to formally reassess the 1956 revolution and to make a clear commitment to the multi-party system; then, in April, he talked the Party into holding a meeting that openly discussed reforms and included a renunciation of "democratic centralism." Finally, in May, he won a commitment to hold an early, special national Party Congress in October, with the prospect of "further personnel changes."

A delicate, unpleasant, and inconvenient situation

As the Hungarian Party was unraveling, there was an unexpected side effect. To the Party's embarrassment, East Germans were taking advantage of Hungary's new era of tolerance. Thousands of East Germans were slipping into the country in order to reach the West through the holes in the iron curtain.

Like many people in the United States, Europeans take long vacations during the summer. Lake Balaton, in western Hungary, is a popular vacation spot for many Eastern Europeans. Summer after summer, thousands of East Germans made the journey through Czechoslovakia to reach Lake Balaton. The Hungarian border guards waved the tourists back across the border at the end of their vacations.

During the summer of 1989, however, more than three thousand East Germans refused to leave. They were waiting in Budapest for permission from the Hungarian government to cross into Austria on their way to West Germany. In fact, more than six thousand East Germans had already managed to cross the border during the summer, passing under the willfully averted eyes of the guards on the Hungarian-Austrian border. In addition to those who declared their intention not to return home, more than fifty thousand other East German tourists were waiting in Hungary.

The situation put Hungary in a difficult diplomatic bind. The government was obligated by a treaty obligation to the Warsaw Pact not to allow East Germans to leave from Hungary or go anywhere but home. Hungary also did not want to offend West Germany, its biggest Western creditor and trading partner, as well as its principal hope for future economic support. As gently as possible, Hungary's leadership called it a problem for the Germans to resolve. They announced, "We find the present situation delicate, unpleasant, and inconvenient." Later in September, it became clear that the Hungarian Communist party was taking a bolder, and a surprisingly unique, position. "Flight from the republic [East Germany]," they said, "is punished by long prison terms and followed by harsh discrimination in professional and social life. Thus we do not wish to feel pressured to forcibly return our visitors."

There is more about the mass exodus of East Germans in the next chapter. It was the crisis that set in motion the elements that would break communism there. For Hungary, it was another event in a long line of revolutionary events. But it was also the moment when Hungary's Communist rulers began to act as a democratic government rather than a puppet government inside the Warsaw Pact.

The last party congress

During its 14th and final Congress, held in October 1989, the Communist party reached several conclusions. First, it had to drop Karoly Grosz from the quartet of leadership and install Rezso Nyers as its new chief. Second, the Party would give itself a new name.

Third, opposition parties had to be legalized. Fourth, the first free elections since 1945 would be held in 1990. Fifth, it would issue a statement condemning the 1956 Soviet invasion, saying, "No power has the right to crush the social and political aspirations of a nation." All together, there were more than one hundred modifications to the 1949 constitution. By a vote of 333 to 5, with 8 abstentions, the modifications were approved.

The Workers Militia, the Communist party's private army of 62,000, was also abolished. It had been created following the suppression of the 1956 insurrection to protect Party members. The militia's continued existence had been a source of profound disgust among the people. "The militia kept feeding the ghosts of 1956," one Hungarian said. New opposition groups had argued that it was "wrong and dangerous for any party to have its own parliamentary force." The Hungarian army lost no time after the Congress, hauling away truckloads of pistols, machine guns, ammunition, and other equipment from the headquarters of the Workers Militia.

On October 23, 1989, five days after the Congress, a special broadcast on national television showed a breathtaking scene. Speaking from the same balcony where, on October 23, 1956, Prime Minister Imre Nagy launched Hungary's extraordinary two-week insurrection, Matyas Szuros, the president of Parliament said that Hungary was now an "independent, democratic, legal state called the Republic of Hungary." The Communist party-state— the Hungarian People's Republic—was dead. Thirty-three years after the insurrection of 1956, Hungary was reclaiming its democratic legacy.

Additional broadcasts of proceedings inside Parliament carried more amazing news. "The history of the Hungarian Socialist Workers Party [the official name of the Communist party] is over," said the announcer. Hungarian Communism was committing suicide on national television. On the podium, before an astonished nation, speaker after speaker denounced the mistakes and horrors of the past and rhapsodized about the miracles of democracy. "It is a time of confessing guilt, accepting responsibility, pledging purification," one leader cried. In an explosion of remorse, the leaders of the past were asking the people of the future for forgiveness. It

Hungary's General Secretary Karoly Grosz and Prime
Minister Miklos Nemeth during a Communist Party Congress
on October 5, 1989. Eighteen days later, the Communist
party fell from power. (AP/Wide World Photos)

was a spectacular performance. Nyers added, "We beg you to
remember that we are Hungarians, too."

Death was promptly followed by rebirth when 1,005 out of
1,202 Party members voted to repackage themselves as the Hungarian Socialist party. Many in Budapest wondered whether this
was not merely new paint on an old facade. After all, this was the
fourth time in its history that the Hungarian Communist party had
changed its name. It declared: "The new party is determined to
face the past of its predecessor with relentless sincerity. The Hungarian Socialist Party disassociates itself from the sins and the mis-
taken principles or methods of the Hungarian Socialist Workers
Party. The new Hungarian Socialist Party fully endorses the universal values of human development, freedom, democracy, and the

respect for productive work." Given that more than 80 percent of the Communist members of Parliament had obediently voted for the makeover, it was a completely ridiculous statement.

Imre Pozsgay

Imre Pozsgay instantly became the moving spirit of the new Socialist party. In fact, he was the best advertisement for the new party's claim that communism could change its stripes. He joined the Party at the height of the Stalinist era in the early 1950s. After a career in the provincial apparatus, he was made minister of culture. He became the main architect of change from within. He was demoted in 1982 to head the Patriotic Front, a small meaningless Communist-controlled umbrella organization. He used the opportunity to build strong ties with the emerging opposition groups, including economic experts and intellectuals. By 1989, he was recognized by many Hungarians as a Communist "worth tolerating." Next to Pozsgay, Gorbachev sounded like the voice of old-fashioned, hard-line communism. "We don't know how this experiment will end," he said at the October Party Congress. "We only know that we had to change. Communism had reached the end of its usefulness."

Sensing the winds of change, Pozsgay admitted: "Of course, the Socialist party wants a leading role. But in the not-too-distant future the government is likely to be a coalition. We need a government of national unity, a strong government of pluralism and democratic principles. The new Socialist party's support of this risks losing—of being voted out of power." In view of what happened to the Communists in Poland's June elections, Pozsgay had reason to wonder. Moreover, polls in November showed that the Socialist party was not attracting new members. In fact, in the first months after the Party Congress, less than twenty thousand people enrolled in the new party. The whereabouts of the other 680,000 members of the former Communist party was a mystery. Some were possibly waiting for the Leninist or Stalinist banner to be unfurled elsewhere. Others may have entered the opposition or abandoned politics altogether.

So why had the Party started a risky course? "Because there is no other way," Pozsgay explained. "Old-style Communist principles have led to a dead end in Eastern Europe wherever they were tried. Now the main difficulty of the democratic transition is a peaceful dismantling of the old structures of the party-state. We have achieved a major step in that direction by changing the Party. The second task is instituting the rule of law, which will provide a new framework for relations between state and society. Then we must build the trust necessary for the introduction of change and I hope the Parliament will support the proposals put forth by the opposition. But the greatest difficulty comes from the depth of our economic crisis. The most urgent task is to create conditions for the development of a market economy."

It was so quiet

"The Hungarian Revolution just happened," said one reporter. "It was so quiet." The events of 1989 were not a remake of 1956. The difference was that Hungarians did not have to fear a Soviet invasion. Mikhail Gorbachev was busy with his own numerous problems; invasion was the farthest thing from his mind. In the words of Hungary's prime minister, "This time our hands were not tied down."

The heroes of Hungary's quiet revolution were also very different from their predecessors of the Nagy era. They did not want a repeat of the bloody suppression of the 1956 insurrection, with its twenty thousand dead and two hundred thousand exiled. In 1989, Hungarians felt a link to the revolutionaries in 1956, but they were wary of the myth of a sudden and radical break with the past. They appreciated the virtues of national unity. Their solution was the gradual rediscovery of democratic politics. What made the transition to post-communism politics peaceful was that the Party acted the part of willing victim, that the oppositionists were democrats rather than revolutionaries, and that society acted like a committed observer rather than an "unbridled force."

The scope of the new freedom was vast and like nothing the Hungarians had experienced in the 20th century. Some scholars

Tens of thousands of people gathered before Parliament on
October 23, 1989 to hear the acting President Matyas Szuros
announce the death of Communist Hungary and the birth of
the Hungarian Republic. (AP/Wide World Photos)

believe that the retreat of the Party was the result of economic
failure and the rising democratic hopes of the people. But was this
enough? Unlike Poland, the floodgates in Hungary were opened
from above—by the Party. The distinguishing characteristic of the
Hungarian Revolution of 1989 was that the Communist party was
able to adapt to and anticipate change—even at the cost of aban-

doning the central ideas of communism. Anything, they supposed, to keep their monopoly on power.

Goulash politics

As East Germany and Czecholslovakia somersaulted and tumbled toward democracy, Hungary continued to quietly transform itself. "Like a caterpillar becoming a butterfly," one Hungarian said. Strangers drifted together to discuss the future. People wanted democracy, that was certain, but wondered how to achieve it. "Yesterday, it was one thing, and today another." Many Hungarians talked about designing democratic institutions that combined the separation of powers and the checks and balances of the United States, a French-style presidency to ensure stability, and the West German electoral system, which seemed the most democratic in its concern for minority representation. As one journalist put it, "Hungary was choosing its democratic dinner from an à la carte menu."

The variety of political parties that flourished after the October 23 announcement suggested that the country was on the right path. In all, there were as many as 50 new political parties. One writer compared the new political scene to Hungary's earlier "goulash communism." He said that the situation resembled "a cluster of competing political boutiques whose merchandise, while stylish, interests no more than a fraction of voters. The essential common touch is hard to find."

There was an unusual mixture of old parties and new parties. Most of the old parties had disbanded after World War II or during the rise of Stalinism. The Independent Smallholders party and the Social Democrats, for example, were brought back to life by many of the same leaders who ran them before 1947. In fact, the average age of the leadership in both these parties was somewhere around 80. This was not a selling point to the millions of Hungarians in search of new ideas. As a result, membership figures were not impressive.

The newer parties attracted more people and were a more vibrant force. Many of the new parties claimed to have inherited the spirit of the opposition movement. The most popular new parties grew directly out of the rising tide of unhappiness that characterized the 1980s. The Democratic Forum, for example, was founded in 1987 as an informal body to discuss the country's most urgent problems. Their first meetings attracted hundreds of spectators. Everyone was surprised that their meetings were tolerated by the government. The Forum's leaders talked broadly about the desire for a free press, free elections, and general reforms. They discussed economic and ecological issues. By 1989, the Democratic Forum had taken advantage of the new openness and grown into a vast intellectual and political movement.

Today, the Democratic Forum appeals to Hungarian nationalism and has the support of many writers and poets who are known as populists. The Forum is outspoken on the plight of the persecuted Hungarian minority in neighboring Romania. It also has raised a number of social issues, such as Hungary's low birthrate, widespread alcoholism, and a suicide rate that is said to be the highest in the world. It attributes all of these troubles to the influence of communism. Its leaders believe that Hungary should not imitate the Western model, but should seek a "third way" between capitalism and socialism.

The Free Democrats, on the other hand, have their eyes on the West. They attract the large middle class of urban professionals. Their 80-page political manifesto published in spring 1989 was noted for its depth and brilliance. But it did not reach a large public. The Free Democrats reject the Forum's belief that there is a "third way" between communism and the West. It is "unashamedly pro-Western." Its manifesto calls for a free market economy based on "unlimited competition and private property." Moreover, they would take Hungary out of the Warsaw Pact.

Free elections

Another hurdle was safely passed in Hungary's transition to democracy in March 1990. The Hungarian Democratic Forum won 43 percent of the votes in the elections held on March 25. The Free Democrats came in second, winning about 24 percent of the vote. Other parties won less than 8 percent, including the Socialists. Imre Pozsgay's hopes for a major role in a new coalition government were obliterated.

From all appearances, the success of the Democratic Forum and the Free Democrats suggested that a majority of Hungarians wanted a center-right coalition, bonded by anti-communism. When he received the news that he had been elected prime minister, Jozsef Antall, leader of the Democratic Forum, wept. "After having gone through the last 45 years, the Hungarian people have cast votes more or less the same way," he said. "This means that after several decades of dictatorship, their historical and political reflexes are not any different. We are still alive."

For the new prime minister, the election was a satisfying victory and a clear vindication of the past. As the child of a prominent anti-Communist and as a young participant in the 1956 insurrection, Antall had been harassed by the Workers Militia all his life. He was subject to periodic arrests and beatings. Until 1974, he was denied the right to travel, even to the Soviet Union.

After his election victory, Antall explained that he would create a coalition government that would include two smaller parties— the Independent Smallholders and the Christian Democrats. Together, this group would command more than 60 percent of the 386 seats in the new Parliament. He added that the Smallholders had won about 60 percent in the 1945 election. "Was it not just and fair," Antall asked, "for history to return the Smallholders to seats in a democratic Parliament?"

What could be expected of Hungary's first democratically elected government since 1945? Naturally, there were all kinds of hopes and fears. Would the Communists, who hoarded millions of dollars, seize control? Would Antall create a good and fair government? Would the Forum's success cause the revival of nationalism and old disputes? Antall said that he was not the leader of a nationalist party. "There are people who want to find a narrow spirit of nationalism and extreme political views among us," he said. According to Antall, the Hungarian Democratic Forum is a "European center party" with strong ties to the other democratic parties, and is committed to returning Hungary to "a new and rational European order."

Antall's government adopted a detailed political program that runs 164 printed pages. Although it did not address all the issues of political and social life, it was a remarkable democratic document. The following are some of the key points:

Political Principles: The National Democratic Forum is a democratic, centrist party, committed to Hungarian traditions. It is not an ideological or class party. It rejects ideologies which aim at the building of socialism. Similarly, it rejects nationalism and chauvinism. It supports a multi-party system of government and embraces the spirit of democratic compromise.

Local Government: Hungary supports self-government. Autonomy will be introduced at village, town, city, and county level. Hungarians must learn to govern themselves democratically, respecting the rights of all people.

Environment: The environment is our greatest resource. The Forum government will work to protect the Carpathian Basin in its entirety. The government will enforce strict measures to protect the environment.

Economy: The Hungarian economy is in a state of profound crisis. The current introduction of a market economy must continue but only so long as the people are willing to support it.

Family Protection: The government has a responsibility to provide people with basic needs if they cannot provide them for themselves. People are entitled to own private property. Women are free to choose whether to stay at home or to work.

Public Health: Public health cannot renew itself without the solution of social and environmental problems. We insist on open competition between the forms of medical insurance and all forms of health care.

Education: The financing of education is the task of the state. Parliament will determine the amount of money to be spent per student, taking into account every type of school. Students must be encouraged to gain a wide area of knowledge and are entitled to the right to select careers of their own free will.

Foreign Affairs: Hungary must accept the universal values of Western civilization. Neutrality is the realistic aim of the future. A neutral Hungary can maintain a stable, partner-like relationship with the Soviet Union as well as develop constructive ties to other nations.

A transition to what?

The small, unthreatening minority of Socialists in the Parliament approved Antall's political manifesto with gritted teeth. In the summer of 1990, Antall's government struggled to rebuild the nation. Not unlike Poland's post-communist government, they faced two fundamental problems. These problems stood between Hungary and real democracy. First, what was the future of the national bureaucracy? Second, what was to be the fate of the local Communist bosses, now called Socialists, in most cities? The Forum government has promised rank-and-file government employees that their jobs are safe, at least for now. Everyone agreed, though, that the senior Communist bosses had to go. The problem was what to do with the massive mid-level bureaucracy who were part of the system but who also possess the skills needed to keep the new government running? More importantly, the local bosses who wielded the real power were still firmly entrenched.

March's parliamentary election did not get to the heart of the old system. Up for election in the next round of voting in 1991 will be the jobs of all the local council members, secretaries of the executive committee, local police captains, prosecutors, and chief judges—a bureaucracy that could involve as many as three hundred thousand people. For the time being, people are afraid to line up against the old bosses. According to one Hungarian, "I know lots of people who want to run but it would be better if the parties could make some sort of agreement about who will run. It will be hard to fight the local apparatus. They are incredibly strong. Real change will not come to most towns for years."

3 EAST GERMANY

One Fatherland

Thousands of East and West Germans celebrate the
beginning of a new year at the remains of the Berlin Wall
in front of the Brandenburg Gate on January 1, 1990.
(Reuters/Bettmann Archives)

A Chronology of Events in East Germany

June 1948	Soviets begin a blockade of Berlin, and Allies respond with an airlift.
August 1961	The Berlin Wall is erected.
May 1971	Erich Honecker becomes general secretary.
October 7, 1989	Mikhail Gorbachev warns Honecker that "life punishes those who delay."
October 9, 1989	Honecker's orders for the police to shoot demonstrators are not obeyed; weekly demonstrations continue every Monday in Leipzig.
October 18, 1989	Honecker is ousted and is replaced by Egon Krenz.
November 5, 1989	Five hundred thousand demonstrators gather in East Berlin.
November 7, 1989	The government resigns.
November 9, 1989	The Berlin Wall is opened; thousands of East Germans visit the West.
December 3, 1989	Egon Krenz, the Politburo, and the Central Committee all resign.

| March 18, 1990 | In East Germany's first free election, 87 percent of the vote goes to pro-reunification parties. |

| October 3, 1990 | The two Germanys are united after 45 years. |

WHEN THOUSANDS OF THE BEST and brightest East Germans fled their country in the summer and fall of 1989, and thousands more inside the country demonstrated for freedom, the Communist regime closed the country's borders. General Secretary Erich Honecker compared the situation to that of China in the summer of 1989 and ordered the police to fire on the demonstrators. From that day forward, the crowds grew week by week in quiet defiance of the government. "Freedom!" they shouted, and very quickly East Germany's Communist party got their message.

The German question

Of all the Eastern European nations, Germany has presented the greatest challenge to both East and West, whether united in a single nation, as it was before 1945, or divided, as it was after World War II. The divided nation was named the Federal Republic of Germany (West Germany) and the German Democratic Republic (East Germany). Historically, Germany has challenged the world in culture, arts, science, and military prowess. Since the rise of the German Empire in 1871, the surrounding European nations have been obsessed with the question of how to deal with this powerful nation that lies at the very center of Europe.

Twice in the 20th century, Germany led the world into war. During World War I (1914–1919), the Germans very nearly succeeded in toppling the French and British governments. An entire generation of Europe's young men were decimated in the fighting. During World War II (1939–1945), the Nazi regime created a huge police and military state. Its goal was to control all of Europe, if not the world. Moreover, the regime was dedicated to the wholesale destruction of all Jews, and more than six million Jews were killed in what is known as the Holocaust. Other Holocaust targets included the Poles, gypsies, homosexuals, and opposition groups from occupied countries. The brutality with which the Nazis killed these people continues to mortify the world.

After 1945, two German nations were established from the four Allied-occupied zones created after the war to restore order to Germany. Great Britain, France, and the United States wanted their occupation zones reunited. The Soviets, however, refused to relinquish control over their zone. "The Soviet bloc leaders," one historian wrote, "justified the division by conjuring up the bogey

Members of the Communist Youth in East Berlin, circa 1950. In the background are remains of the destructions of World War II. (German Information Center)

of the German threat." Thus two German states were created side by side, initially in mutual nonrecognition. These two Germanys that emerged from the ruins of World War II were in every respect unequal. West Germany had more than three times the population of East Germany and more than twice the land area. It was also far richer in natural resources and industrial strength. East Germany became the western anchor of the Soviet empire, and in the years to follow, lagged behind West Germany in most respects.

The Berlin Wall

On August 13, 1961, at 1 A.M., Soviet and East German troops began sealing off the crossing points that tied together East Berlin and West Berlin. Clusters of troops gathered at each crossing point, with machine guns, armored cars, and tanks. The entire 28-mile border, running through the heart of the city, was sealed. Before daylight, squads of workers arrived and trucks delivered rolls of barbed wire, iron posts, and slabs of concrete. Over the next few days, desperate East Berliners tried to escape—rushing across the barbed wire, jumping out of windows on the border, smashing through the barriers with homemade tanks. The opportunities for escape were few and soon eliminated. Every exit was suddenly slammed shut, every window that butted the Western border was bricked, and within a week, West Berlin was completely shut in. It is important to realize, however, that although a wall surrounded West Berlin, the real prison was in the East. "The people of West Berlin were free," one East German wrote. "They could travel, vote, and buy whatever they wanted. We were the ones trapped by the Wall."

Festooned with enough barbed wire to circle the globe, the Berlin Wall came to symbolize the cold war. As a background for y stories, Berlin became the scene of memorable exchanges be-een East and West secret agents. It also became the scene of ng escapes by brave men and women, some hidden in com-ments in trucks and cars, some escaping by hot air balloons, thers still making midnight dashes through the sewers beneath

East German troops on display on one of East Berlin's boulevards. This 1969 rally honored those who died in the fight against Nazi Germany. (German Information Center)

the city. Many escapes ended in gunfire and death. Along the length of the Berlin Wall, small shrines were placed with names or photographs of those who did not get away.

The Berlin Wall was actually made up of two walls separated by a frightful forbidden zone, or no-man's-land, marked by a series of watchtowers, electrified fences, barbed wire, and land mines. On the East Berlin side, patrols with dogs watched every person who dared to get close to the wall. West Berliners detested the wall, but they learned to live with it. Over time, they jogged along its length, and painted it from end to end with graffiti. But except for those rare places where it is coldly visible, or on rare occasions when some important politician came to make a speech beside it, they tried to forget it. East Berliners could never forget the wall. Eighty people died trying get over it.

East Germany under Erich Honecker

When Erich Honecker rose to power in 1971, he was often reduced to pressing the claim that East Germany was more authentically *German* than West Germany. Born into a family of poor coal miners, he grew up hating the inequalities of capitalism. Honecker became a communist when he was a teenager. In 1935, when Honecker was 23 years old, Hitler's security force, the SS, arrested him and sentenced him to ten years in prison. Honecker was not released until the end of the war in 1945. He joined the Central Committee of the Communist party in 1946, the Politburo in 1950, and became general secretary in 1971. Because of his belief that the communist end justified any means, Honecker defended his role in building the Berlin Wall in 1961, describing the edifice as "an antifascist barrier" against West Germany. One writer concluded, "Given his experiences under Nazism, Honecker believed a lie." All his life he maintained that the Nazi epoch was a direct, natural consequence of the "evils of capitalism" and that, in spite of its flaws, communism represented a significant historical advance.

After he became leader of East Germany, Honecker began to forge a somewhat unique economic program. It was not as radical as Hungary's "goulash communism," but he made some industries less dependent on government ministries. He also relaxed restrictions against the Protestant church, and let more East German citizens visit relatives in the West. These measures helped him preside over the country's transformation into an industrial and military power, second only to the Soviet Union in the Warsaw Pact. At last, it looked as if East Germany, like West Germany, had created its own economic miracle, expanding to the maximum capabilities of the two competing systems implanted after the war.

Resisting *glasnost*

When Mikhail Gorbachev became general secretary of the Soviet Union in 1985 and began to introduce reform, Honecker could not adapt. He continued to compare capitalism and communism to "fire and water." Gorbachev recognized that the communist economic system was a failure, but Honecker refused to abandon central planning and expensive subsidies on basic consumer goods. "When I went to meet with Honecker," said one of his former economic advisers, "he was very much aware that 85 percent of the West German population had a higher living standard than us, but he also knew that 15 percent of them live in extremely poor conditions. Honecker believed we had a responsibility to take care of that remaining 15 percent, whatever the cost."

In addition to turning a deaf ear to *perestroika*, or economic reform, Honecker's government had no interest in *glasnost*, or openness. Dissidents and political rivals were thrown into prisons. One ex-prisoner explained that life in prison was not different from life anywhere else in East Germany, except that "prison was more interesting." Criminals, he added, were set apart from political prisoners. Criminals got special treatment and favors—more visitors, more food, and the easy prison jobs like working in the laundry or dishing out food. Political prisoners had yellow stripes on their sleeves and pants, and they were all there, he said, "with the idea of being innocent."

The Party's reluctance to embrace Gorbachev-era reform was a mixture of conservatism and self-satisfaction. According to chief ideologue Kurt Hager, who said in April 1987, "You don't need to change the wallpaper in your apartment just because your neighbor is doing his place up." The editor of a Communist journal added, "The Soviet Union has won great historical merit for having defeated Hitler and won the war, but as far as technology and progress is concerned it is no model for us."

Fearful of the sweeping changes in the Soviet Union, Poland, and Hungary, the East German authorities even banned the Soviet magazine *Sputnik* as well as several Soviet films. As a further insult to the people, Honecker heaped honors on the brutal regime of Nicolae Ceausescu. Although both Poland and Hungary had embarked on the road to democracy, East Germany remained unmoving. Honecker declared that the Berlin Wall would stand for another fifty or hundred years if necessary, to protect "our republic from robbers." East Germans could only despair.

In a growing atmosphere of frustration, many East Germans, especially young people in their twenties, submitted applications for emigration. A young woman explained her long journey: "I started making plans when I finished high school. I knew my application would sit around in East Berlin for five, six years. I wanted to leave legally, but all I got for trying was threats from the one secret police agent and a job offer from another. I knew I would have to leave illegally." For many, there seemed to be no way out except individual attempts to escape. When a college student was shot and killed while trying to cross the forbidden zone on February 6, 1989, no one realized that he would be the last person to die on the Berlin Wall.

The exodus

Before the November collapse of the Berlin Wall, 1989 had seen the largest illegal exodus of East Germans since the wall was built. People fled, not across the wall into West Berlin, but through new holes in the barbed wire iron curtain that separated Hungary and Austria. The massive exodus was a humiliating loss to the Communist regime and important in its downfall.

The iron curtain first began to crumble on March 19, 1989, when Hungary became the first Eastern bloc country to sign, albeit 38 years late, the 1951 United Nations Convention relating to refugees. The convention's operative principle, which Hungary's new, reform-minded leaders embraced, was that no refugees should be returned against their will to a country where their life or liberty would be threatened. This was in direct contradiction to a treaty signed by Hungary and East Germany in the 1970s. The Hungarians had their own reason for signing the United Nations document. They were not about to return more than ten thousand ethnic Hungarians who had fled Romania's campaign of forced assimilation in 1988.

In May 1989, the Hungarians began to tear down part of the barbed wire fences and watchtowers that formed the iron curtain on the Austrian border. Word quickly spread to East Germany that it was possible to walk across the border from Hungary into Austria. From there, people heard, it was even easier to reach West Germany, where East Germans would receive automatic citizenship.

In summer 1989, a flood of East Germans escaped into Western Europe through Hungary when Hungary began dismantling its iron curtain border with Austria. (Reuters/ Bettmann Archives)

It was not an easy option. Much of the barbed wire was still intact, and Hungarian troops still patrolled the border. The lucky ones made it through the woods and swamps, evading the soldiers (who sometimes, but by no means always, looked the other way). By August, more than two hundred East Germans were crossing into Austria every day. Those who were caught could console themselves with the fact that they were free to try again. Many, unable to get through the border and rapidly running out of money, sought refuge in the West German embassy in Budapest. Between May and August, more than six thousand East Germans crossed the border illegally from Hungary into Austria.

Honecker demanded that Hungary close its borders to Austria. "The Hungarian people are bound by treaty and socialism to the people of East Germany," he warned. The East German government also responded to the crisis by limiting the access its citizens had to Hungary. Hungary-bound travelers were stopped and thoroughly searched. Anyone traveling light was deemed to be making a one-way trip and sent back. Shrewd travelers began booking round-trip tickets to destinations like Bulgaria, and traveling with baggage as if on a family holiday—only to make an unscheduled stop in Budapest. Other East Germans began showing up at the West German embassies in Prague and Warsaw. Both Czechoslovakia and Poland were countries East Germans could enter without too much difficulty. The numbers, small at first, kept growing. By September, more than seven thousand East Germans waited in West German embassies in Prague and Warsaw. In Budapest, more than twenty thousand refugees were waiting for Hungary's permission to leave the country, and the numbers kept growing.

At the stroke of midnight on September 13, Hungary finally decided to no longer observe its treaty with East Germany. The western border with Austria was now open. A stream of freedom-seekers turned into a flood. In three days, thirty thousand people passed through the Hungarian-Austrian border. Some people had spent weeks preparing for the trip. Others made the move at the last moment. One young woman described how she and her boyfriend decided to leave after hearing on the radio that the East Germans in Budapest had been allowed to leave. She said they rushed to her parents, and her parents told them, "You go on. We would do the same if we were young and had the possibility."

Honecker's government became even more resolved to seek the return of the East Germans who were flooding Prague and Warsaw. First, he closed the East German borders. Then Honecker said he would guarantee permission to emigrate to those refugees who returned to East Germany first. Very few people agreed to these conditions. Finally, on October 1, after frantic negotiations among East Berlin, Prague, and Warsaw, the refugees were permitted to seek refuge in the West. West Germany's foreign minister, who had himself fled East Germany in the 1950s, appeared on the embassy balcony in Prague and made the announcement: "You are free to follow the lives you wish!" By October 4, more than seventeen thousand East German refugees had been taken by train from Prague and Warsaw to the West German border. Many reports described how thousands more flocked to stations and junctions along the railroad line. They, too, wanted to leave. Many tried to sneak aboard. "Conditions became so hectic in Dresden," one reporter wrote, "that police had to clear the terminal by force and seal the doors of the trains from the outside to block them."

For the East Germans who remained behind, the summer of 1989 was a time of enormous frustration. Each evening, they saw

Only weeks after General Secretary Erich Honecker celebrated the 40th anniversary of East Germany on October 7, 1989, he was ousted from power and placed under house arrest. (AP/Wide World Photos)

television images of East Germans streaming across the Hungarian border to Austria. Then they saw thousands crowding into West German embassies in Poland, Czechoslovakia, and Hungary. Faced with this crisis, Honecker behaved as unbendingly as ever. The state-controlled media vilified the young refugees as "traitors, for whom we will not shed a tear."

The struggle to oppose

As thousands of East Germans showed their disillusionment with the Communist regime by choosing to emigrate, even greater numbers stayed to wage a peaceful revolution. Unlike Poland, there was no strong, organized opposition in East Germany. (There also were no Communist leaders like Imre Pozsgay of Hungary who were willing to talk about reform.) Nonetheless, there were many dissidents. Some of them began an organization called the New Forum. "Our only purpose," one Forum member said," was to help organize the people. We distributed leaflets telling them where the next rally would be. We spread the word. That's all. We did not want to become a political party."

The absence of a German Lech Walesa or mass movement like Solidarity did not mean that the East Germans were any more satisfied with their government than the Poles. On the contrary, the continued decline of the economy and the government's unwillingness to reform built up enormous frustration. "We no longer believed the endless lies of the Party," one East German explained. "It was so obvious that leaders were completely isolated from the mood of the people."

Like the Roman Catholic Church in Poland, the Protestant churches of East Germany helped support the opposition. In addition to providing moral support, they provided a place where people could meet to talk in relative safety. As a result, many church-related opposition groups blossomed. Working with the New Forum, East Germany's churches helped dissidents collect and expose evidence of vote fraud by the Communists. In one East Berlin district, church-based poll watchers interviewed voters and recorded five times the 1,600 negative ballots counted by officials. The church even dared to demand a government investigation of its fraud charges. It was no accident that the Gethsemane and Zion churches in East Berlin and the Saint Thomas and Saint Nikolai churches in Leipzig became the rallying points of East German's revolution. In August and September, Leipzig was the setting for East Germany's most reliable anti-government demonstrations. Every Monday, large numbers of people gathered for the "peace service" in Saint Nikolai Church. Filling the church to capacity, people stood in the aisles and outside in the church courtyard. The services attracted all types of independent-minded individuals. "Many were not faithful believers," a parishioner explained. "But we were united against Honecker's handling of the emigration crisis. Some of us came to Nikolai because it was the only place to get truthful information."

After the service, demonstrators spilled out on to the streets of Leipzig. Several hundred usually ended up at Karl-Marx Platz, a student organizer said, "wondering what to do and what to say. It was easier to complain inside the churches than it was on the open square. We felt so vulnerable." Another protester explained, "I have two teenaged children. They both want to go to West Germany. How can I stop them? There is nothing here for them; this is not a country to enjoy life in." She went on, "I have never protested before. None of us ever had the courage, but I have to do something for my children, or they will leave." As Mondays came and went, and the numbers of demonstrators increased, people gathered courage. They began to make it clear that they wanted to enjoy Gorbachev-era reforms. They also began to demand freedom of travel.

Most East Germans supported the people of Leipzig, but were still unwilling to march in their own streets. By late September, "peace services" were being organized in other cities, including Dresden and East Berlin, but the subsequent marches attracted only a few thousand participants. One reporter wrote, "The demonstrations appeared like a few brilliant flashes of light on an otherwise darkened East German map." But if East Germany's peaceful revolution had an epicenter, it was in the city of Leipzig, where

Hundreds of thousands of citizens demonstrate against the Communist regime in the city of Leipzig, demanding freedom and a reunited Germany. (German Information Center)

the crowds were already chanting the inevitable slogan: "Germany, united Fatherland!"

Gorbachev's advice

As the opposition marches slowly gained momentum and their numbers increased, Honecker struggled to resolve the emigration crisis. Despite the growing tension, the Communist party went ahead with its plans to celebrate East Germany's 40th anniversary. On Saturday, October 7, as part of the state-sponsored festivities, more than one hundred thousand members of the Communist youth group Free German Youth rallied in East Berlin, and a military parade was staged. Thousands of red flags hung from buildings. Patriotic music and socialist slogans were amplified through the streets. Mikhail Gorbachev attended and was cheered by the crowds who—as it turned out—had gathered mostly to see him.

As Honecker and Gorbachev saluted the parade, protesters clashed with the police and security forces nearby. They chanted "Gorby! Gorby!" Others shouted, "Perestroika!" According to some reports, many members of the Communist youth organization broke with the official march to join the protesters and cheer Gorbachev.

Before his departure that evening, Gorbachev was reported to have given Honecker a bit of advice: "Life punishes those who delay."

The demonstration in Plauen

East Berlin was not the only city that experienced anti-government demonstrations on October 7. Spurred on by the presence of the Soviet leader, protesters gathered in many other cities, including Leipzig, Dresden, and Plauen. These demonstrations attracted the largest-scale unrest in East Germany since a failed workers' uprising in 1953. Crowds reached into the tens of thousands. The largest and most unified rally occurred in the industrial city of Plauen, located less than 20 miles from the West German border. Up to a quarter of its eighty thousand citizens defied heavily armed state power on that gloomy anniversary.

Rumors and leaflets had been circulating around Plauen for days. Everyone "knew" an unofficial demonstration would start at 3 P.M. on October 7 in the central square. Police and city administration were also aware of plans to disrupt this national holiday, but as a police colonel admitted, they expected no more than 40 "counterrevolutionaries" to gather in the center of town. Unwisely, local officials refused to cancel plans for a Communist-sponsored "people's festival" that afternoon, and could not legitimately stop anyone from entering the downtown area. By the appointed hour, thousands of people, young and old, from all walks of life, found themselves standing around uneasily at the city's center, under a steady stream of rain. In the sea of thousands of people, there were only three or four homemade banners, hastily written on bed sheets and fastened between umbrellas. One banner read: "For reforms and freedom to travel—but above all for peace."

Most would-be demonstrators were unsure exactly why they had come. Some would later claim simple curiosity had driven them. A high school student said, "We were all afraid. It was the kind of thing you would come to with your best friend, since you distrusted everyone else—the stranger next to you might be from the secret police. But we all knew that if a demonstration started we would not just stand around watching." A young metalworker recalled, "We all knew we were going to a demonstration, even if there were a lot of curiosity-seekers. But when we all got there we were very nervous, and hoped someone would do something."

The first to break the tension was a young man from a local school. He climbed on top of a small stone statue next to a theater and held a sign reading, "We want Freedom!" He was quickly joined by another student who raised a black-red-gold West German flag. The crowd applauded and began to chant, "Germany! Germany!" Suddenly a man dressed in a trench coat forced his way through the crowd, ripped down the flag, and punched its carrier in the face. At this moment, according to one spectator, the crowd became unified. "In this moment we felt the unity of shared rage."

Slowly, but with increasing strength, chants rose from both ends of the square: "Gorby! Gorby!" "Police go home!" and "Reform!" Two lines of police armed with truncheons and shields tried to force the demonstrators back into side streets, but soon found themselves surrounded by the immense crowd. Aided by church members, the alarmed, mostly young, police officers retreated. On the opposite end of the square, two fire engines commandeered by the police indiscriminately blasted the crowd with water. Police jeeps and fire engines drove directly into the crowd, hoping to disperse it. But by now the mob was enraged. It responded with a hail of bottles and stones, forcing the police aggressors to withdraw. The crowd shifted across the square to city hall, which was sealed off by rows of riot police, machine-gun carrying militia, and regular police with unmuzzled dogs. As the masses converged on city hall, clashes erupted. The police line surged forward repeatedly, beating the people with truncheons. A police helicopter flew at rooftop level, darting through the air above the crowd.

Thomas Kuttler, a prominent Protestant churchman, was in the crowd. Fearing that greater violence could explode at any moment, Kuttler made his way through the police lines into city hall. He knew the mayor and would ask him to come out and calm the crowd. The scene he encountered was one of disarray. "City officials nervously smoked one cigarette after another, while some disassembled chairs to make clubs for themselves, apparently expecting some sort of last stand." The gap between the rulers and the ruled was never more striking, Kuttler later recalled. At first, the mayor was unwilling to leave the safety of city hall, yet after repeated coaxing by Kuttler, he seemed prepared to address the crowd. Just as he was about to step outside with Kuttler, a security official pulled the mayor aside. After a short conversation, the mayor returned to inform Kuttler that under no circumstances would he leave the building. The mayor was no longer in charge. Kuttler assumed that orders were arriving from district Party headquarters in Karl-Marx-Stadt.

Senior city officials encouraged Kuttler to address the crowd. "Calm them," they begged. Standing awkwardly behind a row of police on the top of the stairs in front of city hall, Kuttler tried to make himself heard. The crowd chanted, "Megaphone, megaphone!" and soon one was brought to him. He told the crowd, "You have made clear the intentions of your demonstration. These have certainly been heard. But now this demonstration should have a peaceful ending. The mayor is prepared to talk with you, even if he cannot do so now. I myself will try to see to it that talks take place. It is painfully clear that our society urgently needs changes. The main thing is that there be no violence." The crowds applauded and cheered the churchman.

Later that evening, after the crowds abandoned the square, troops were called into Plauen and instantly cleared out and sealed off the center of town. In the course of this action, 92 people were arrested, many of whom had been simply coming home from a concert or movie. They spent the night chained together under pouring rain in the local prison's courtyard. Most were released the next day, but a few were held in solitary confinement for several days.

The next day, a furious Honecker telegraphed district first secretaries of his Communist party. He said that unapproved demonstrations had occurred the previous day in several cities. "Especially in Dresden, Plauen, and Leipzig they assumed the character of mob riots and violent excesses that have disturbed our citizens to the highest degree," he said.

A mood of awakening

In Leipzig, where the weekly peace service was expected to draw a large crowd on October 9, tensions ran high. Churchgoers had to brave riot police, soldiers, and secret agents to gather at Saint Nikolai. "When word got out that the police were hanging around the church and that riot police were stationed in the square, more people showed up," said one Leipzig resident. More than seventy thousand people turned out. According to East Germany's former spy chief, "There was an order from Honecker for a Chinese solution. It could have been worse than Beijing."

As the critical moment approached, prominent Leipzig citizens and Party officials met to discuss ways of preventing a deadly confrontation between the unarmed peace demonstrators and the powerful security forces. Meeting at the home of Kurt Masur, an internationally celebrated conductor, they managed to diffuse the situation. When the masses of people marched in the streets that evening, the police did not intervene. "From that day forward," one spectator wrote, "the crowds in Leipzig grew week by week, some seventy thousand, double that, three hundred thousand, and then, five hundred thousand. Our revolution was finally taking place."

On October 18, the Communist party leadership ousted Honecker. "There was no resisting the revolutionary tide," admitted a former high-ranking Communist. "Under Honecker's leadership, the Party was losing its authority and socialist order was being undermined." Honecker's legacy was soon shattered. The Party that he helped found not only removed him and 11 top associates from power, but expelled them, placed them under house arrest, and indicted them for corruption and abuse of power.

The East German Politburo installed Egon Krenz, a hard-fisted Honecker disciple, as Party chief. Krenz made himself instantly visible to the people in factory meetings and street crowds, pleading for public acceptance as a reformer. "The situation in East Germany is loaded with tension and is highly contradictory," he said. "There is a mood of awakening that has never been known until now."

Addressing a large, unfriendly crowd outside Communist party headquarters, Krenz offered his vision of the future. "We want a socialism that is economically effective, politically democratic, morally clean, and most of all, has a face turned to the people." In short, Krenz wanted a socialism that had never existed in the Soviet bloc. Concession followed concession. By late October, Krenz's government reopened its borders with Czechoslovakia, proclaimed an amnesty, or pardon, for all those who had left, and promised that travel restrictions would be eased, or abolished, by Christmas.

Meanwhile, thousands of East Germans once again poured out of the country through Czechoslovakia and Hungary. Three hundred thousand demonstrators gathered in Leipzig on October 30, and five days later, half a million East Berliners showed their opposition to the regime. "The Party could no longer control the events," said a former Communist. "It could no longer rely on the police or army to obey its orders, and when the Party leaders tried to address the crowds, they were shouted down."

The Wall falls

The last times Berlin made major headlines in the news was during the Berlin airlift after World War II and when the Berlin Wall was built in 1961. Thereafter, one German wrote, "Berlin was simply a schizophrenic city. A remnant of a vanished metropolis, occupied by conquerors—in the West a prosperous fortress of two million people; in the East a prison house its masters called paradise, a place of outer darkness." An historian wrote, "Berlin was not a

In East Berlin, demonstrators gather to protest the Stalinist policies of the Honecker regime. (German Information Center)

place—it was an issue." It never quite seemed to be part of modern Germany. When people thought of West Germany, they tended to think of Bonn, its capital city, of Mercedes and BMW, and of the strength of the deutsche mark.

Then suddenly the world stood on its head. On November 7, 1989, the East German government resigned, and the following day, Krenz announced the resignation of the entire Politburo and the formation of a new government. On November 9, the East Berlin Party leader, Gunter Schabowski, gave an evening press conference that was televised live. He casually announced that "permission will be given at short notice for private travel and permanent emigration without the present preconditions having

In early November 1989, as East Germans march in the
streets, West Berliners show their support by climbing and
hacking away at the wall that divides their city. To the
astonishment of the world, the Wall was finally opened on
November 9. (Reuters/Bettmann Archives)

been fulfilled, across all border crossing points between East and West Germany, and East and West Berlin." By midnight, tens of thousands of people were pouring through the wall to West Berlin, their first opportunity in 28 years. West Berliners rushed into the streets to welcome them.

On Friday, November 10, both East and West Berliners began smashing through the Berlin Wall. Young people from East and West climbed on top of the wall and showered each other with champagne. By November 14, there were 22 new crossing points, with promises of more to come. Each day, huge numbers of grateful East Germans poured through these gaps. "As the Cold Warriors predicted, there was an invasion from the East," one West Berliner said. "But the invaders carried shopping bags instead of Soviet machine guns, and they arrived not in tanks, but on foot!"

The people of West Berlin delighted in the face of this invasion. Cinemas gave out free popcorn. The Opera House offered a free performance of Mozart's *Magic Flute*. City officials allowed free travel on the subway, the U-Bahn. They gave each new arrival 100 marks to spend. The department stores hung out welcome signs. Around the square in the center of West Berlin, sausage stalls, trestle tables, mobile toilets, street musicians, and information booths appeared.

There were some people who did not approve of this mass family reunion. An English reporter recalled how a taxi driver worried out loud about the cost of it. "After all," the driver said, "there are at least a million East Berliners, and at 100 marks a head, the overall subsidy for this invasion, in every sense, is not small beer." Similarly, non-German workers were worried. "What will happen to me?" the Turkish cleaning woman of a block of apartments asked her employer, "when the people of East Berlin undercut me?" Her employer admitted that three offers had already been presented.

Others worried about the presence of Soviet armies nearby. Wasn't the wall a crucial and heavily symbolic border? Fifty miles to the east, the entire Polish nation worried. They had remarkably sad memories of the last united Germany. Moreover, why had the West German chancellor, on a recent visit to Poland, refused to state that the postwar borders with other countries were immovable?

(The Allies gave Poland large areas of German land after World War II.) "It was all very confusing and very euphoric and vaguely troubling all at once," said one Berliner. "We all hoped this would happen one day but we never imagined it could happen so quickly."

The Party disintegrates

The opening of the Berlin Wall signaled the collapse of Communist East Germany. The Party's disintegration continued at a steady pace. On November 13, Hans Modrow, the Party leader from Dresden, was made prime minister. Modrow was one of the few Communist leaders who retained any popularity. He had kept up a dialogue with the opposition in Dresden, and had met demonstrators there. Working together, Modrow and Krenz struggled to gain the confidence of the people. On November 22, however, the country was scandalized to discover the affluent lifestyle of Honecker and other Party leaders, past and present. Reporters had been allowed to inspect the government compound in Wandlitz, north of Berlin, where 23 top leaders and their families had lived in luxury.

The special privileges enjoyed by the Communist leaders were a considerable annoyance to the East German people. Few of them were prepared for the stark truths. Television images of Wandlitz showed heated swimming pools, tennis courts, beauty parlors, a cinema, fully stocked shops, and elegant restaurants. In a country where people waited years for a two-room apartment and where law forbade citizens from taking more than seven dollars across the border, stories surfaced of hunting retreats stocked with deer and spacious houses fitted with expensive tiles and wood, purchased abroad. Moreover, the funds to pay for these luxuries had been embezzled from state industries. One Party official's wife was said to have ordered an Italian tile floor only to have it ripped up again and redone. Another Party official reportedly used a government jet to fly his family to the United States for vacations. Often the revelations were not overwhelming by Western standards, but in East Germany the public was shocked. Their anger fed the demonstrations. "We really didn't expect this corruption," one East

German said, "We really thought these people lived simply. It's like having 25 Watergates all at once."

Krenz, who had a house in Wandlitz, could not defend himself, and on December 3, at an emergency meeting, the entire Politburo and Central Committee resigned. Krenz lost the job he had won from Honecker only six weeks earlier. A Party Congress three days later elected Gregor Gysi to replace Krenz as Party chief, and a new government, headed by Hans Modrow, the only Party leader to survive the cataclysm. Free elections were promised in the spring.

The wheels of reunification

The drama of East Germany's revolution galvanized the desire for a reunited Germany. Helmut Kohl, the West German chancellor, stood on the steps of West Berlin's city hall after the Berlin Wall was first breached and proclaimed, "I want to call out to all in the German Democratic Republic: we're on your side, we are and remain one nation. We belong together!" Critics thought it was wrong to plant such seeds. Heiner Muller, a respected East German playwright, spoke for many East Germans when he said, "I do not crave one fatherland; I do not seek reunification; I have not protested for this." Muller, though not a supporter of the Communist government, was an eloquent critic of the "way of the West." He wanted, like many other East Germans, to create a new country with a non-capitalist government. According to Muller, "Capitalism leads to catastrophe, as it produces ever more meaningless things, at greater speed."

The new Communist leaders announced that "reunification was not on the agenda"—as it was not on the agenda in many European capitals. There were 16 million East Germans and 62 million West Germans; upon reunification there would be 78 million "new" German citizens. These figures haunted nations who had been bullied by Germany before. Nonetheless, reunification was sure to happen. A French diplomat explained, "When we expressed our concerns, the Germans begged for our trust. Instead of preventing them, the Allies and victors of the Second World War seemed to permit reunification." Prime Minister Tadeusz

Mazowiecki of Poland gave his reluctant support, "It is hard for me, being a Pole, to desire a powerful German neighbor; nevertheless, the people of East Germany deserve to choose their own course after having lived with the horror of four decades of Communism and with the appalling lies of Yalta."

The ground swell for reunification was widespread inside the two German states. According to Radio Free Europe's polls released in February 1990, 87 percent of the East Germans and 81 percent of West Germans wanted reunification. East Germans were so impatient that two thousand of them left for the West every day, draining the country of skilled labor. Meanwhile, West German and East German allies were dragged along, bewildered and slightly nervous. Where were the loyalties of a country that belonged to both NATO and the Warsaw Pact? This, obviously, was a real sticking point. The question was what price could the Soviet Union extract from the West for removing its troops from eastern Germany and accepting a united Germany that was tied to NATO.

In other matters, the problem was less the new rules than the old rulers. Just as in the aftermath of World War II, there were many hundreds of thousands of people who served the dictatorship in one way or another. This list included not just Party and state bureaucrats, but lawyers, teachers, professional soldiers, police, and the *Stasi* (State Security Service). For example, what should be done with the more than sixty thousand full-time employees of the State Security Service? Could they simply go on living in a unified Germany, settle down to enjoy a comfortable retirement on a West German pension? Bonn's answer is a new law that states that anyone who was "significantly involved" in repression is not entitled to a pension. But how does one determine "significant involvement"? How, above all, without working through the estimated nine miles of files in the *Stasi* headquarters in East Berlin? But the information in those files, including the names of many informers, could tear society apart. The files could reveal, for example, that one's neighbor or even family member had collaborated with the *Stasi*.

The reunification problems that caused the greatest concern, however, were the economic and social ones. Both East Germans and West Germans were asking themselves, "How much will it cost us?" For the West Germans, the cost would come in the straightforward form of higher taxes, competition for jobs and housing, and a weakening of the currency. For the East Germans, the challenges were much more fundamental: unemployment, drastic inflation, and much higher standards in the workplace.

Compared to the situations in Poland and Hungary, the wealth and interests of West Germany were an immense advantage. Yet this advantage also produced unique problems. In all the formerly communist countries, there was the difficulty of trying to turn state-controlled property back into private or at least cooperative property. But in Germany, many of the former, prewar owners (or heirs) lived in West Germany. If East Germany simply adopted West German law, then hundreds of thousands of West Germans would start reclaiming their property. The East German press, for example, published many horror stories of West German landlords turning up in their Mercedes and threatening to quintuple the rent overnight.

A grand coalition

East Germans had their first free elections since 1932 on March 18, 1990. The electorate widely approved of reunification. The Christian Democrats, who supported reunification, won 48 percent of the vote. The Social Democrats and the Liberals won a combined 28 percent of the vote. The former Communist party (renamed and repackaged) won an unexpected 16 percent. However, as one reporter explained, "none of these totals takes into account the 400,000 East Germans who had already voted against Communism with their feet" by moving to West Germany.

On April 12, East Germany's new, non-communist government reached an agreement to form "a grand coalition" government including Christian Democrats, Social Democrats, and Liberals. Lothair de Maiziere, head of the Christian Democratic party, became prime minister. He announced that the chief task of the new government would be "to lead the nation to union with West Germany." The coalition government achieved the two-thirds majority in the new Parliament needed to make changes in the constitution. This was the last major obstacle to the start of formal negotiations with West Germany on unification. Maiziere also promised to initiate meetings between the two Germanys and the four Allies of World War II.

Only peace will emanate from German soil

On September 12, 1990, the four wartime Allies who defeated Nazi Germany 45 years earlier signed a treaty to relinquish all their occupation rights. The treaty signing concluded meetings known as the "two-plus-four negotiations." With a beaming Gorbachev standing behind them, the foreign ministers of West Germany, East Germany, France, Great Britain, the United States, and the Soviet Union took turns signing the treaty. Then the six leaders clinked glasses of champagne in a toast to the end of Europe's postwar division. "September twelfth," the Soviet foreign minister said, "will go down in history as a date important in many ways for both Europe and the world at large." Gorbachev added, "We are going through emotional and historical events. We have drawn a line under World War II and we have started keeping the time of a new age. May it be peaceful and prosperous." James Baker, secretary of state of the United States, said, "Let our legacy be that after 45 years, we finally got the political arithmetic right. Two plus four adds up to one Germany in a Europe whole and free."

The East German revolution had finally resolved the "German question" and put an end to the last formal remnants of occupation. The Allied leaders restored full sovereignty to a nation that had savaged Europe. In exchange, the Germans renounced all claims to ancestral lands east of the Oder and Neisse rivers lost to Poland and the Soviet Union, agreed to restrict their military, and pledged that "only peace will emanate from German soil." On October 3, 1990, after 45 years, the two Germanys were reunited with jubilation and a vow of peace.

4 CZECHOSLOVAKIA

The Ten-Day Revolution

A young protester in Wenceslas Square during a general strike against the Communist government. (AP/Wide World Photos)

A CHRONOLOGY OF EVENTS IN CZECHOSLOVAKIA

May 1948	The Communist-dominated National Front wins an electoral victory.
January 1968	The beginning of the Prague Spring.
August 31, 1968	Soviet troops lead a Warsaw Pact invasion of Czechoslovakia.
March 1969	Gustav Husak becomes general secretary.
January 1977	Charter 77 is circulated.
December 1987	Husak is replaced by Milos Jakes.
January 15, 1980	Five thousand demonstrators in Prague's Wenceslas Square commemorate Jan Palach's suicide in 1969; Vaclav Havel and other dissidents are arrested.
November 17, 1989	Anti-government demonstration in Wenceslas Square is brutally broken up by police.
November 19, 1989	The Civic Forum is created in the Magic Lantern Theater.
November 20, 1989	More than two hundred thousand people protest in Prague; demonstrations continue and grow daily.

November 24, 1989	Alexander Dubcek returns to Prague; Milos Jakes and the Communist leadership resign.
November 27, 1989	The Civic Forum directs a two-hour general strike in support of democracy.
November 28, 1989	The Communist party promises to hold free elections and to abandon its "leading role."
December 7, 1989	The government resigns.
December 10, 1989	A new government with a non-Communist majority is formed.
December 29, 1989	Vaclav Havel is elected president.
June 8–9, 1990	The Civic Forum wins 48 percent of the vote.

N DECEMBER 1989, graffiti appeared in Prague that went like this: "Poland, ten years; Hungary, ten months; East Germany, ten weeks; Czechoslovakia, ten days." In a region where history was frozen for four decades, it moved with startling rapidity in November 1989. In the words of Vaclav Havel, the new president of Czechoslovakia: "The moment someone breaks through in one place, when one person cries out, 'The emperor is naked!'—when a single person breaks the rules of the game, thus exposing it as a game—everything suddenly appears in another light and the whole crust seems then to be made out of tissue on the point of tearing and disintegrating uncontrollably."

The next domino

The first Eastern bloc country to throw off the shackles of communism was Poland, now governed by a prime minister who is not only non-communist, but also, very precisely, anti-communist.

Next in the overthrow of communism was Hungary, where the Communist party, in the course of renaming itself, seemed nearly to abolish itself. Next in line was East Germany, where walls of every kind were torn down. And sooner than anyone expected, the people of Czechoslovakia, in their millions, joined the marvelously peaceful revolution that was transforming Eastern Europe. The evolution of the Czechoslovak opposition movement broke all records. In ten days, it achieved what Poland's Solidarity took nearly ten years to extract: a commitment from Communists, accustomed to jailing their critics, to abandon the Party's monopoly on power. The communist world was shaken apart without bloody coups, without violence.

This great uprising transformed the minds of the Czechoslovakian Communist party members. Only a few weeks before the revolution, they had been faithful servants of Gustav Husak's totalitarian leadership. By December, it was hard even to find a Communist. "If these gray-suited bureaucrats were singing a different tune," wrote one Czech, "it was because they were forced to by the people who could no longer bear their arrogance."

As thousands of people gathered night after night in Prague's largest square in late November, the Communist leadership threatened to impose martial law. On November 22, Prime Minister Ladislav Adamec waved away the opposition. To him, the dissident playwright Vaclav Havel was no one at all, "an absolute zero." Yet when Adamec tried to speak to the largest crowd ever assembled in front of Party headquarters, they were chanting Havel's name, not his. Ten days later, it was left to Adamec to parrot the unfamiliar phases by which the Communist bureaucracy hoped it could retain some shred of power and privilege.

A relationship with the Soviet Union

When Czechoslovakia gained its independence after World War I, the new national boundaries joined two Slavic groups—the Czechs and the Slovaks. As a nation, it emerged from the ashes of a 19th-century empire better prepared for independence than any of the other new Eastern European countries. As this was the most industrially developed area of the former Austro-Hungarian Empire, the country's people benefited from the presence of established industries and a literate, large, prosperous middle class. Czechoslovakia enjoyed 20 years of open, democratic, and libertarian government that were unrivaled anywhere in Eastern Europe at the time. Over 20 political parties represented political opinions, nationalities, and religions during the period of the First Republic. In 1938, when Hitler rolled his armies into Czechoslovakia, the democratic government collapsed.

Six years later, on May 5, 1945, the people of Prague finally rose up against the retreating Germans. But neither the Czechs nor the Slovaks could liberate themselves. They needed the help of the American and Soviet armies. General George Patton of the United States reached Plzen, within striking distance of Prague. His superiors, concerned about the agreement made at Yalta with the Soviets, forbade him to liberate the capital. Instead, Soviet troops arrived in Prague on May 9, 1945.

Unlike the Poles, the Czechs and the Slovaks looked upon the Soviet Union as a friend. A successful Soviet-backed Communist Party existed in prewar Czechoslovakia and achieved a large membership and considerable respect. Moreover, the Soviet Union was the only power in 1938 that had declared its readiness to aid Czechoslovakia. When Soviet troops entered Prague in 1945, masses of people and red flags welcomed them.

After the war, the Czechs and the Slovaks worked together to rebuild their democratic government. In an attempt to recreate the former peace, Eduard Benes was invited to return to Prague and reoccupy his position as president. Benes had been president of Czechoslovakia when the Nazis invaded. Like many other government leaders, he fled to England and spent the war years presiding over the government-in-exile. His first official act upon returning to his ravaged country was to invite the old political parties to reemerge and prepare for free elections.

The Communist party won about 40 percent of the vote in the 1948 free election. It was the greatest showing of support the Communist party ever received in Eastern Europe. Communists participated in the new government, holding 8 out of 25 posts. Over a period of months, they increased their pressure. What happened next is a matter of dispute. Did Moscow order its Czechoslovak comrades to seize power? Or did the Czechoslovak Communists act themselves? It began when the Communist minister of interior launched a purge of the police. In defiance, the non-Communist ministers resigned. Benes accepted their move and let the Communists name replacements. Democracy suddenly vanished. In the words of one Czech writer, "Czechoslovakia abruptly changed from a socialist democracy into a Stalinist state of horror."

The Prague Spring

In the years that followed, Czechoslovakia turned into a hard-line and loyal Soviet ally. Only once, during the "Prague Spring" of 1968, did it break the mold and move towards greater freedom. Communist party leaders themselves, led by Alexander Dubcek, promised "socialism with a human face." Interestingly, their ideas would later inspire Mikhail Gorbachev, the Soviet leader who invented *glasnost* and *perestroika*. But in 1968, it was not Gorbachev but Leonid Brezhnev who occupied the seat of power in the Soviet Union. On August 21, after months of threats, Soviet troops invaded and occupied Czechoslovakia. They were accompanied by the armies of the Warsaw Pact nations, including East Germany, Poland, Hungary, and Bulgaria. Faced with such overwhelming odds, the Czechoslovaks offered little resistance.

After the invasion, Gustav Husak was made president of Czechoslovakia and leader of the Communist party. Husak was an unusual choice. In 1954, the Communist party charged him with "bourgeois nationalism" and gave him a life sentence. Released only in 1960, he was readmitted to the Party in 1963 and fully restored to honor that year. In 1968, Husak was a respected government official and supported the Prague Spring. Thus, many Czechoslovaks approved the choice in the hope that Husak would stand up to the Soviets. He did little to justify their trust, however. Husak soon purged Prague Spring reformers from the Party. He banished Dubcek from Prague, placing him in a minor government job in Bratislava. Many others, including some of the country's most promising writers and artists, were forced to leave the country forever.

Husak held on to power for more than 20 years. In 1985, when the more youthful Gorbachev visited Husak in Prague, they strolled through the old city together. The Soviet leader plunged into crowds, shaking hands and smiling to the cries of "friendship, friendship." The white-haired Husak walked a few steps behind him, "stiff and stern," according to one Czech, "a stubborn relic from another era." Finally, in 1987, Husak lost his position as general secretary of the Communist party to Milos Jakes. Husak, however, continued to serve as president of Czechoslovakia.

Charter 77

Freedom of assembly, a basic human right, was strictly limited by Czechoslovakia's government. Like other Eastern Europeans under communism, the Czechoslovaks turned to opposition groups after realizing that traditional political activity was doomed to failure. In 1977, a document called Charter 77 was signed by 241 Czechoslovaks and marked the beginning of an opposition movement. The signers came from diverse backgrounds—liberals, democrats, Protestants, Catholics, Jews, communists, reformers, and even some who considered themselves revolutionary Marxists. Charter 77, however, never claimed to be a mass movement. By its own description, the Charter was "a loose, informal, and open association of people of various shades of opinion, faith and profession united by the will to strive individually and collectively for the respect of civil and human rights." It had no platform or political program. Vaclav Havel, one of the Charter's first signers and Czechoslovakia's best known dissident, described the movement as "an icebreaker with a kamikaze crew." Its essential purpose, Havel declared, "was active defense of human rights."

Both the problems and the strengths of the Charter were exemplified by Vaclav Havel. A slight, soft-spoken playwright of enormous courage, Havel spent five years in prison, where he nearly died of illness. His plays were banned in Czechoslovakia for 21 years. His prominence as an artist and his persistence against the state made him the symbol of dissent. Yet, through the years of persecution, Havel, like the Charter, was more a spokesperson of conscience than a political activist. "I do not intend to take for myself the role of professional politician," he declared as students chanted his name in November 1989. "I have never had that ambition."

In addition to defending human rights, Havel and the other signers of the Charter spread their interests to encompass threats to the environment, religious and ethnic rights, social and economic problems, and the rights of artists. At its peak, the Charter had about two thousand members. All had signed its founding document. Signing was an act of courage because the consequences could be harsh: official harassment, loss of jobs, house searches, endless interrogations by the secret police, crude pressures against close relatives. Security guards once broke into Havel's apartment and dumped quick-drying cement down his toilet.

Sparks of defiance kept spirits alive. Even high school students showed their support of the Charter. After the death of John Lennon in 1980, for example, students painted tributes to the slain ex-Beatle on the wall under Prague's Charles Bridge. "John Lennon loved the Charter," someone scrawled. Someone else wrote, "You have your Lenin, Give us our Lennon." Police quickly slapped white paint over the graffiti.

Opposition in the 1980s

Before Czechoslovakia's revolution began on November 17, 1989, opposition activists were mulling over their past and future. Their principal achievement, as veteran dissident Jiri Dienstbier said, had been preserving the moral will to resist: "We were passing a small candle through the darkness." The movement's major failing had been its inability to spark protests across Czechoslovak society. The massive demonstrations in East Germany caused only ripples in Czechoslovakia. As long as Husak and the party-state appeared invulnerable, people remained complacent. "In my opinion this society was completely destroyed by the Communists," wrote the editor of an illegal underground publication. "It is truly appalling. People want democracy but they do not want to pay for it."

Dissidents complained about the lack of a central opposition organization. Though united under the spirit of Charter 77, they lacked a concrete, alternative political program. Moreover, they did not seem to be closing the gap between the Prague-based intelligentsia, which guided the opposition, and the rest of Czechoslovakia's 15 million people. Many leaders of Poland's Solidarity opposition built their legitimacy as representatives through years of close contact with the working class. In fact, many in the Solidarity leadership had come from small towns. But the writers, actors, artists, and journalists of Czechoslovakia's opposition functioned mainly as a moral beacon for a demoralized society.

The government continued to do everything possible to break the opposition and to keep them from becoming a united force. It usually refused to acknowledge the opposition's existence. When it did acknowledge them, the dissidents were branded as creations of the "Western media and human rights groups." Members of the Communist party who joined and supported the Prague Spring movement were purged from the Party after the Warsaw Pact invasion. They and other oppositionists found themselves stoking coal, cleaning bathrooms, and driving taxis. Their children met mysterious difficulties when they attempted to get into college. Their telephones and apartments were bugged. They lived, as ever, under the constant threat of interrogation, searches, and jail. Police were assigned to them like case workers, following them everywhere, noting the names of people who went in and out of their apartments. Fear of such punishments limited the number of Czechoslovaks willing to join the intellectuals and artists. Not surprisingly, the independent groups had to concentrate more on mere survival than on developing a political program.

By the late 1980s, independent activism had spread in other directions, far beyond the expectations of Charter 77. Widely circulated petitions called for the release of jailed dissidents and an open discussion of the 1968 invasion. Demand grew for underground publications. Thousands of Catholics flocked to pilgrimages with anti-communist undertones. Former associates of Alexander

Dubcek, the father of the Prague Spring, formed *Obroda*, a self-described "club for socialist restructuring." Dubcek himself emerged from his isolation, calling for a Czechoslovak *perestroika* in interviews with the Western press.

By the late 1980s, a younger generation of students and workers helped to retrench the opposition movement. Free of their elders' defeatism, the students freely expressed their frustration with the authorities' refusal to accept Gorbachev-era freedoms. A Slovak writer explained that "they rejected the unwritten social compact by which the Communists filled store shelves in exchange for the acceptance of the regime's hard-line government." High school and college students formed more than thirty new opposition groups and began to link up with the older dissidents. A group called the "Czech Children," made up of young adults in their 20s, joined in demonstrations for political freedoms and environmental protection. The "John Lennon Peace Group" grew out of informal meetings that advocated the rights of musicians and other artists. And the "Society for a Merrier Present," armed with cucumber and salami truncheons, staged mock police assaults on demonstrators in Prague.

On January 16, 1989, a small group of high school students made their way, peacefully, towards the statue of Vaclav, the good king Wenceslas, at the top of Wenceslas Square. Exactly 20 years earlier, a student named Jan Palach had set himself on fire to protest the Soviet invasion. Before the students could commemorate his sacrifice, police began using water canons and tear gas on the crowd. Within moments, the calm square was transformed into a tear gas-filled battle zone. Off to the side, Vaclav Havel watched the scene in horror. When he tried to leave, a plainclothes security guard grabbed him and threw him into the back of a police van. Intent on making an example of Havel, the regime staged a harsh show trial in February for his role in the demonstration. The prosecutor claimed Havel had incited the demonstrations by giving interviews to foreign radio stations. In fact, Havel had warned the students against using violence to press their grievances. "I consider the way I am treated as an act of vengeance for my ideas," he told the court. The judge sentenced Havel to nine months in prison.

Remember this day

Ever cautious, the people of Czechoslovakia watched the Poles vote the Communist government out of office in June 1989. They watched again as the Hungarians and the East Germans achieved freedom.

A demonstrator is detained by riot police in Wenceslas Square in Prague for shouting anti-government slogans. This was a common scene throughout Eastern Europe in Fall 1989. (AP/Wide World Photos)

The enormous mass movement that overthrew Czechoslovak Communism rose up with amazing speed. By the last week of November 1989, millions of people had participated in demonstrations across the country. It was only a month before, in late October, that dissidents were able to bring about a street demonstration involving ten thousand people. These brave souls had scarcely unfurled their pro-democracy banners before truncheon-wielding police chased them through the streets of Prague. Three weeks later, in late November, hundreds of thousands of demonstrators were routine in Wenceslas Square. In a matter of days, they brought down the Communist leadership and dispatched the Party into permanent oblivion.

Charter 77 and the long-persecuted dissident community deserve much of the credit for the dramatic turnaround. But news reports of the revolution often overlooked the role of Czechoslovakia's high school and college students. On Friday, November 17, more than fifty thousand students turned out for a demonstration to mark the 50th anniversary of the murder of a Czech student by the Nazis. It was a long, joyful march, with chants and slogans directed increasingly against the present rulers of Prague Castle— the seat of government power. Marching toward Wenceslas Square, the protesters shouted, "Dinosaurs, resign!" and "Communists, get out!" When the marchers reached the square, hundreds were surrounded and cut off by the white-helmeted riot police and, for the first time, by red-bereted anti-terrorist squads. The students placed candles before them and tried to give them flowers. They knelt on the ground and raised their arms, chanting, "We have bare hands." But the police, and especially the red berets, beat them nonetheless. Wave after wave of the berets charged at them with flailing white truncheons.

The regime's decision to use force was a monumental blunder. Milos Jakes, the new Communist party boss, hoped it would frighten the students back into passivity. But the dramatic liberalizations of the Soviet Union, Poland, Hungary, and especially East Germany had primed the population for rapid change. The zeal with which security forces bloodied unarmed students shocked Czechoslovaks more than any event since Soviet tanks rolled over the Prague Spring reforms 21 years earlier. It shattered the passivity that had long frustrated dissident organizers. "This is the start of the finish of the government," one man shouted during the violence. "The people will remember this day!"

In the streets of Prague, impromptu shrines, tended night and day, lighted the spots where students fell. Candles, flowers, and photographs commemorated each encounter. A massive circle of candlelight at the foot of the towering statue of King Wenceslas illuminated the night in honor of the 1969 martyr Jan Palach. "Now the ghost of Palach," said one Czech, "along with the old hero-king Wenceslas, and a little help from Vaclav Havel, will stir our country."

Prague ignites

The awful parallel between the regime's violence against student demonstrators and that of the Nazis exactly 50 years earlier created an immensely powerful emotional rallying point. This was the spark that set Czechoslovakia on fire. With reports of one student dead, and scores in the hospital, the students were determined to do something. On Saturday, November 18, student leaders decided to call a nationwide general strike in a week's time. The students were soon joined by people who worked in the theater. Theater people, including actors, directors, set designers, and writers, knew how to organize themselves. They had spent years rallying support for their favorite playwright, Vaclav Havel. On Sunday, November 19, Havel himself called a meeting of all the main opposition groups in the Magic Lantern Theater. They joined together in what they called a Civic Forum.

The Civic Forum soon became the united voice of the opposition. But it was Prague's high school and college students who were showing Czechoslovakia the way. A few moments after the first meeting of the Forum began, Havel rose from his chair. "Thanks to the bravery of the students, we are gathered here. The students have finally cast off the timidity and fear of our people." A few days later, another Czech explained, "For 20 years people kept quiet and knuckled under for their children's sake. And now

Vaclav Havel addresses an overflowing crowd at the Magic
Lantern Theater. Havel, an internationally renowned
playwright, was soon to find his place in the political history
of Czechoslovakia. (AP/Wide World Photos)

the police were beating even the children." A banner hung high
during Sunday's rally said, "Parents come with us, we are your

children." And so they did. On Monday afternoon, a crowd of more than two hundred thousand people filled Wenceslas Square.

By the middle of the week, the center of Prague was plastered with homemade posters declaring "Truth will prevail!" and "Let the government resign!" Groups gathered in front of shop windows where televisions played over and over again a videotape of the November 17 brutality. Even larger groups gathered for the afternoon demonstrations in Wenceslas Square. People waved the distinctive Czechoslovak flag—a blue triangular field at the left, with a band of white and a band of red on the right—and chanted away as if it were the most usual thing in the world. Cars honked in support as they drove across the square, and small children gave the V-for-Victory sign. "The excitement fed upon itself, crossing all social boundaries," wrote one journalist. The demonstrations drew people of all ages and interests. "Longhaired musicians," she reported, "stood shoulder to shoulder with beefy steelworkers." Knots of people gathered on street corners to debate the future.

If Prague was in the grip of euphoria, it was partly because tragedy had been averted. For days it looked as though the regime might opt for martial law. As the demonstrations in Wenceslas Square grew larger, Jakes threatened on national television to "introduce order." The government ordered members of the workers militia to take up positions in Prague. Uniformed police occupied the city's radio and television stations. The state-controlled television called on citizens to "protect socialism." Rumors flew. But the authorities appeared to lack the will to use force. They ordered the police to withdraw from Wenceslas Square. They even promised to investigate allegations of police brutality. Then, Prime Minister Ladislav Adamec met with members of the Civic Forum for the first time. He promised, "There will be no more martial law."

The return of Dubcek

Alexander Dubcek stepped off the 9 A.M. bus from Bratislava on Friday, November 24. He looked, according to one writer, "as if he had just stepped straight out of a photograph from 1968. The same gray coat, the same tentative smile, the same hat. It all contributed to the illusion that we had just left a 20-year timewarp, with the clock that stopped in 1969 starting again in 1989." By nightfall, according to another writer, "Dubcek had almost the stature of a shadow head of state." In Wenceslas Square, young protesters knew the 68-year-old former leader from the yellowing photographs that hung in Czechoslovak living rooms for two decades. When Dubcek stepped out into the frosty evening air, illuminated by television spotlights, the crowd gave an enormous roar: "Dubcek! Dubcek!" The old leader smiled and thanked the crowd for welcoming him. Then he asked, "Wise men said once there could be light, so why now should there be darkness?" People wept and cheered.

As Dubcek spoke, the leaders of the Communist party were holding an emergency meeting in a distant suburb. During a 16-hour meeting, Jakes was facing an inevitable dilemma: to declare martial law and crush the protest movement with force—possibly at the cost of hundreds of lives—or to give in to the popular will and resign.

Later in the evening, Dubcek and Havel shared the stage of the Magic Lantern Theater, headquarters of the Civic Forum. "Beginning tomorrow," Havel declared, "we must begin a dialogue with the authorities. I don't know whether they will allow it, but the agenda is clear: we want democracy, we want to rejoin the European community." As the two leaders talked about their different ideas of socialism to the overflow crowd, a messenger carrying remarkable news interrupted them. Jakes and the rest of the 13-member Politburo were stepping down. To succeed Jakes as Communist party general secretary, the Central Committee named Karol Urbanek. Though Urbanek was not well-known, the change brought a tremendous relief. "The pressures for change were so vast," said one Czech opposition leader. "People feared that the old hard-line government, if not changed, would have led the country into civil war."

According to a spectator at the Magic Lantern that evening, the theater "erupted" when the news was read. People applauded and cheered, some sobbed for joy. Havel embraced Dubcek and made the V-for-Victory sign. Someone jumped on the stage with bottles of champagne. Havel raised his glass and toasted a free Czechoslovakia.

Jingle your keys!

At a rally the next day, more than five hundred thousand people braved the bitter cold to gather at Prague's Letna field, outside a huge sports stadium. It was the biggest rally in the country's history, broadcast live on national television. Addressing the gathering, Havel begged the Czechoslovaks to continue to put pressure on the government. "Power once again passes to the neo-Stalinists. Who is Urbanek? We are not satisfied. We will gather and protest until we *are* satisfied." When Havel told the crowd that Prime Minister Adamec had allied himself with the Civic Forum and might be the best man to form a new government, the crowd responded with the enthusiastic chant: "Adamec, Adamec, Adamec."

They roared with joy again when Dubcek appeared: "Dubcek for President, Dubcek for President!" The masses serenaded him, singing "We wish you long life" and urged him to "take the Castle." Again there were cries for the government to resign, expressions of support for the general strike scheduled for Monday, and most important, cries for free elections. Leaders from the Civic Forum addressed the crowd. One speaker suggested that "the general strike act as a referendum on whether or not we want to go on being humiliated and also whether the leaders of the one political party, permanently monopolizing the leading role, should continue to ruin this country."

The scene was repeated on Sunday. This time, Prime Minister Adamec was invited to address the crowd. When he started to demand more "discipline," no more strikes, and economic rather than political change, the people were stunned. They glared at Adamec. A few people started jingling their keys. There were shouts: "People! Jingle your keys!" Suddenly, half a million people were taking out their keys and jingling them. The people cheered after the noise swept Adamec from the stage.

The general strike

On Monday, November 27, at exactly noon, lights went off and doors clanged shut in offices, restaurants, cafes, bookstores, factories, and schools. Millions of Czechs and Slovaks walked off their jobs. Rivers of people flowed down boulevards and into main squares throughout the country. In Prague's Old Town Square, hundreds of young women with babies gathered around the statue of Jan Hus, the religious reformer. Opposition leaders had sent them there, where they could be protected, lest the babies be hurt in the crush elsewhere.

The Czechoslovak flag hung from balconies, fluttered from poles, and decorated windows everywhere. Flag-colored ribbons were pinned to every lapel and even to the collars of dogs. On every window, even in the state-controlled shops, signs announced: "General Strike!" In the old quarter of Prague, high school students marched beneath school banners. At the Inter-Continental Hotel in the Old Town, the students hauled down the foreign flags in the courtyard and ran Czechoslovak flags up all ten poles. A convoy of taxicabs, lights on and horns honking, snaked through the capital. In Bratislava's main square, people danced. Strikes occurred in the smallest villages, even in the far corners of the country.

By the start of the general strike, it was already clear that it would be a success. The media, including the state-controlled television, gave it extensive and mostly positive coverage. Although most managers at television and radio stations were Communist party members, they were apparently willing to risk their careers. In fact, as the television carried reports of large and peaceful strike meetings from all over the country, a crawl ran across the bottom of the screen: "The employees of this television station support the General Strike. Showing these reports is their contribution."

On Monday evening, yet another crowd gathered in Wenceslas Square. Civic Forum leader Vaclav Havel told the people: "If Adamec does not accept the demands of the people, we will demand the government's resignation." The massive crowd chanted instantly, "Resignation! Resignation!" Havel added, "We have come so far!" Only ten days earlier, government security police

Czech citizens in Wenceslas Square, in memory of the
November 17 police massacre of protesting students.
(AP/Wide World Photos)

were hitting students over the head in the same square. Now the
opposition, having organized a massive, nationwide strike with great
success, was presenting a program for the end of communism in
Czechoslovakia. And the once-reluctant Havel seemed to find his
voice—and to accept his political role—after the week-long national
drama at Wenceslas Square.

The role of the Civic Forum

The Civic Forum, which did not even exist before the November
crisis, moved into the political vacuum almost overnight. Its sudden
founding, just two days after the police beatings, showed that mem-

bers of many different opposition groups were willing to come together. Previously, Czechoslovakia's opposition groups, though supporters of Charter 77, had been disorganized. Unlike Poland's Solidarity, they were not a mass movement. With the eruption of revolutionary fervor in November, they emerged to seize the moment by displaying an unsuspected mastery of coalition politics. In little more than a week, the democracy movement was transformed from a disorganized collage of voices into an organized and eloquent opposition. "We are no longer the opposition," a Civic Forum spokesperson said on the evening of the general strike. "The Communists are the opposition." From then on, the Civic Forum rode a tidal wave of popular discontent.

From its creation, the Civic Forum's role was—to use Havel's favorite characterization—improvised. The Forum made specific demands: that those Communist leaders tied to the Warsaw Pact invasion step down; that an independent investigation of the November 17 police brutality be launched; and that all political prisoners be freed. After the first mass protest, Forum representatives opened talks with the more reformist—and opportunistic—Adamec, securing from him a pledge against further police or army intervention. At first, Havel declined to urge people into the streets; that call came from the students. Yet one day later, he was encouraging a huge crowd in Wenceslas Square to keep up the pressure on the government. Any lingering hesitation to act had been overwhelmed by the revolution "from below." The Forum's "improvisation" was taking its cue from the action in the streets, not from the cooler, calculated decisions of the Prague intellectuals.

As the mass demonstrations continued, Civic Forum's organizational skills rapidly improved. It was increasingly able to channel, if not control, the public outpouring. From its headquarters in the Magic Lantern Theater, it organized the later protests and led the general strike. Just as significant, it was able to halt the mass rallies after Monday's strike in order to conduct power-sharing talks with government leaders in a calmer atmosphere.

The Czechoslovak disgust with communism became so noticeable that even the Party shivered. Faced with such a powerful opposition, the once all-powerful Communists were humbled, offering concessions and self-criticism in vain attempts to appease the crowds who were calling for the end of the system. One of the more amazing developments came on December 1, when the Czechoslovak Communists moved to condemn the very act that gave them authority. "We are of the opinion that the entry onto our territory of the five armies of the Warsaw Pact in 1968 was not justified, and the decision to do so was wrong," said Urbanek. After the announcement was made, Soviet President Gorbachev acknowledged in a press conference that the 1968 uprising resulted from a "yearning for democracy." The new governments of Poland, Hungary, and East Germany had already presented formal apologies to the Civic Forum for participating in the invasion. "It was our dearest wish to fight for your freedom and not against it," the letter from Poland read.

By December 5, it was clear to even the Communist leaders that their monopoly on power was near an end. Finally, the Party leadership accepted the need for a transitional coalition government with non-Communists. The Civic Forum was given grudging recognition by the new Communist party chief, Karol Urbanek, as a legitimate negotiating partner. The goal of the coalition government, from the Forum's perspective, was "to secure fair, multiparty elections and constitutional guarantees of free speech, free press, and freedom of association." The Forum added that it was their plan to dissolve after the elections and let the various political parties do their work.

A changeable coalition

The pressing question was who would serve on a coalition government. Although the Forum was not insisting that its members be named to a coalition cabinet, it claimed a veto power over those appointed. It promptly exercised that veto when Adamec, apparently restrained by the Communist party, tried to weasel out of his promise to share power with non-Communists. On December 6, he announced a new cabinet in which only 5 of 21 posts were given to non-Communists. The opposition called another mass demonstration and threatened a second general strike unless the cabinet was recast to reflect the influence of the opposition.

Vaclav Havel and former Prime Minister Alexander Dubcek
during a reception in December 1989. (AP/Wide World
Photos)

On December 7, Adamec suddenly stepped down, and the
following Sunday, December 10, Czechoslovakia installed a new
cabinet. For the first time since 1948, the Communists were in
the minority. President Gustav Husak, a symbol of the disgraced
old regime, swore in the new ministers before he also resigned.
Vaclav Havel was swept into office as president of the republic on
an irrepressible wave of public enthusiasm. At Havel's express re-

quest, the Parliament also restored Alexander Dubcek to a position of honor as its new presiding officer.

As the euphoria of November and December gradually faded, people set about the task of living in a democracy. Every day, thousands of people passing the Civic Forum's headquarters walked between two huge pillars. The pillars were plastered with newspaper clippings, photographs, and posters depicting life in Czechoslovakia between 1945 and 1989. The effect of this was to remind them of what they already knew—that they had to part with the Communist party. The Communist party was not yet extinct, but it was fast becoming invisible. Marian Calfa, the new prime minister selected to replace Adamec, promptly resigned from the Communist party. Calfa promised free and democratic elections for Parliament, possibly by the end of June 1990. The new leaders agreed that it would take at least that long for the opposition parties to organize, write their programs, nominate candidates, and plan their campaigns.

New faces, new politics

Czechoslovakia had no political life outside the Communist party since the coup of 1948. The first deputy prime minister of the new coalition government was Jan Carnogursky. He personified the "new politics." Two weeks before he took office, the 45-year-old lawyer from Bratislava had been put in jail for demanding free elections. He belonged to Public Against Violence, a Slovak opposition group. The new foreign minister, Jiri Dienstbier, also served time in prison for dissident activities. In recent years, he made his living by stoking a boiler and devoted his free time to the human rights campaigns of Charter 77. Dienstbier was a prominent journalist before the 1968 invasion. He had to persuade a friend to replace him in the boiler room before he could attend the swearing-in ceremony of the new cabinet.

Perhaps the most unusual member of the new cabinet was the minister of labor and social affairs, Petr Miller. Like Poland's Lech Walesa, Miller was an electrician. Real members of the working class were rare among the leaders of the Civic Forum. Recalling his first meeting with the dissidents, Miller told one reporter: "They were looking for representatives of different social groups. Someone said, 'We need a Catholic,' and one was found. Then someone said, 'We need a worker,' and they said, 'Take Miller.' " He turned out to be an invaluable ally of the dissident intellectuals, artists, and students who took part in the creation of the Civic Forum. Miller startled them by delivering on promises to bring ten thousand workers into the center of Prague to join their demonstrators. Delivering a speech for the first time in his life, he rallied Czechoslovakia's working class. They shared his indignation over the brutal police beatings and flooded the streets to stand alongside the students, intellectuals, shopkeepers, and artists of Prague.

Havel and other opposition leaders originally conceived of the Civic Forum as a Czechoslovak version of East Germany's largest opposition group, New Forum. It was to be neither a political party nor an alternative government. Just the same, the Civic Forum quickly found itself pushed beyond negotiating the terms of a dialogue with the government to conducting a dialogue. Thus, the Forum abruptly decided to act as a political party, much like Solidarity did in Polish elections in June 1989. Forum leaders announced that they would endorse candidates to run against the Communists. No other group was in a position to use the people's power in the streets to negotiate concessions from the government.

A colorful campaign

Despite the colossal popularity of the Civic Forum, many new political parties emerged during the first months of 1990. Political life would no longer be divided between the Communist party and the Civic Forum. In fact, by late April, 46 political parties had registered with the new government. Of these, 23 managed to obtain ten thousand members, which entitled them to take part in the upcoming elections. To achieve a seat in the new parliament, however, parties had to win at least 5 percent of the votes cast. The serious contenders for major representation in parliament were the Civic Forum, the Christian Democratic Union, the Green party, the Socialist party, and the Communist party.

The people of Czechoslovakia entered the political arena with gusto. One reporter commented that the new political life of the country was more like a "circus." She wrote that people "were simply too jubilant to fear the hard questions about their political futures." She explained that even the new palace guards could not keep a straight face. "At the Castle," she wrote, "the new palace guards, in their red, white, and blue uniforms designed by an Oscar-winning designer, couldn't take themselves seriously: their stony faces kept breaking into grins as they went through the motions of changing the guard."

The campaign was colorful. Villagers were lured into political rallies with promises of free goulash, childrens' puppet shows, and appearances by heartthrob movie stars. In front of the Civic Forum's headquarters in Prague, there was something for everyone. Celebrity folksingers and jazz musicians performed along with punk-rock groups. There were reports of a wonderfully talented all-boy punk group that wore dresses and had compact discs dangling from their ears. Children passed out buttons with the Civic Forum's smiley face logo. In Slovakia, Forum supporters passed out lollipops and balloons. They put up posters featuring the Smurfs and Mickey Mouse. One poster showed Mickey Mouse thinking, "Yuck, I hate Communism."

As the Civic Forum climbed in the polls, other parties invented similar tactics. The Christian Democrats, whose pious posters featured gentle children bathed in golden light, gathered an army of young blond women with teased hair, tight miniskirts, black high heels, and the party emblem on their backs to pass out campaign buttons. The Socialist party, fading badly in the polls, plastered the city with its own posters just days before the election. "This is it," read the caption, above which a blond woman holding the party emblem smiled brightly in a soaking wet T-shirt. Thanks to the students, not a single Communist party poster could be found anywhere in Prague. Just one banner hung well out of reach on a building in the middle of Prague. The banner pleaded: "There is no democracy without pluralism and no pluralism without the Communist Party." Ironically, after the election, the building became a museum of totalitarianism.

When election day came on June 8, 1990, the Civic Forum

won 48 percent of the vote. Communist candidates were soundly defeated and Czechoslovakia entered, in the words of Vaclav Havel, "an era of national rejuvenation." He added, "Now it is up to us alone whether our hopes come to pass, and whether our civic, national, and political self-confidence reawakens in a historically new way."

5 ROMANIA

December 1989

A statue of Lenin is pulled to the ground in Bucharest in celebration of the collapse of Communism. (AP/Wide World Photos)

A CHRONOLOGY OF EVENTS IN ROMANIA

November 1946	A Communist-dominated front takes control.
July 1965	Nicolae Ceausescu becomes general secretary.
August 1977	Miners in the Jiu Valley strike over living standards and pension cuts.
November 1987	More than ten thousand people demonstrate in Brasov.
March 1989	Human rights activists send an open letter of protest to Ceausescu.
July 1989	Ceausescu plays host to Warsaw Pact leaders.
December 15, 1989	The first demonstrations take place in Timisoara.
December 17, 1989	Ceausescu orders the army and police to shoot demonstrators in Timisoara; thousands are killed.
December 21, 1989	Ceausescu addresses a rally in Bucharest but is shouted down by protesters.
December 22, 1989	Thousands of people storm government buildings in Bucharest; Ceausescu and his wife escape by helicopter.
December 23, 1989	The National Salvation Front emerges, headed by Ion Iliescu, a former member of the Communist Central Committee.

December 25, 1989	Ceausescu and his wife are executed.
March 11, 1990	The Timisoara Proclamation is announced.
May 20, 1990	Ion Iliescu of the National Salvation Front is elected president, winning 85 percent of the vote.

AT THE END of the miraculous fall of 1989, Romania, on the footsteps of the other Eastern bloc countries, exploded. Europe's last Stalinist dictator began to lose control with reckless speed. Nicolae Ceausescu had governed Romania for 24 years. His iron-fisted regime was the longest running in Communist Europe. As Poland, Hungary, East Germany, and Czechoslovakia established new democratic governments, Romania, too, was unable to resist the cry for change. The map of Cold War Europe was shedding its totalitarian skins.

Unlike the other Eastern European revolutions, the revolution in Romania was violent. It resulted not only in the replacement of a hated ruling family, but also in the end of all party and government structures. Bereft of power and authority, communism simply collapsed, ingloriously. The Communist party had essentially disappeared the moment a helicopter lifted Ceausescu and his wife from the roof of the Central Committee building on December 22, 1989.

Ceausescu's flight signified the end of more than four decades of brutal Stalinism. His fall completed the extraordinary cycle of revolutions in Eastern Europe in 1989. In some ways, it was the most important of those transforming events. Of the Eastern European Communist leaders, only Ceausescu tried to crush the popular forces that rose against him. His failure invalidated the first principle of life in the Communist world—the belief that in the end the Party has the means to force the people to submit.

Romania's humiliation

As has been seen in preceding chapters, there was something utterly insufficient about the Communist systems of Eastern Europe. Whole populations—Poles, East Germans, Hungarians, and Czechs—made huge sacrifices for having been born in the totalitarian half of Europe. But, of the citizens of the countries looked at so far, Romanians got by with even less. Conditions in Romania were miserable during the "Epoch of Light," the "Golden Age," as President Ceausescu modestly referred to the period of his rule. Not only were their shops less full, their lives were held back. Even dreams were foreshortened; too often daily life was a nightmare.

Peasants had to travel to towns to find food; in winter people had to cook in the middle of the night because there was no gas during the day. People spent many hours each day lining up for the most basic food and household items, frequently discovering that none were available. Monthly rations of meat, cooking oil, and sugar were often cut without any explanation. Men were taxed if they and their wives failed to produce children. Old people, especially from rural areas, were routinely denied medical treatment. To avoid high infant mortality rates, officials did not register births until children were six months old. In a country once infamous for its antisemitism, the office of the Chief Rabbi displayed a notice saying, "We do not accept conversions" because converts were seen as would-be emigrants to Israel. Underscoring the false promise of the Communist system, Ceausescu built an amazing boulevard celebrating his achievements, carved through the heart of old Bucharest, its central fountains turned on only when the dictator went by in his Soviet-built limousine.

Food and fuel shortages left the population malnourished and shivering in their apartments; Orwellian political repression was part of daily life. After the collapse of the Ceausescu government, a French reporter asked, "What was it like to live under Ceausescu?" The Romanian answered, "It was a system that didn't destroy people physically—not many were actually killed; but it was a system that condemned us, condemned us to a fight for the lowest possible level of physical and spiritual nourishment. Under Ceausescu some people died violently, but an entire population was dying."

Stalin's legacy

Romania was different from other Eastern European countries because it had never undergone de-Stalinization. It had never gone through the process of moving from the absolute rule of one man to the slightly less absolute rule of a communist politburo. To Westerners, the distinction between these two forms of oppression may seem irrelevant, but it is very significant to the people who live under them. A single absolute ruler, in the mold of Stalin, Mao, Castro, or Ceausescu, means a rule unchecked and unmoderated in its arbitrariness and potential for cruelty.

A politburo, on the other hand, even one made up of brutal individuals, provides a moderating check against the worst characteristics of any one member. Compare, for example, Stalin's rule to Khrushchev's. The former terrorized not only the whole of society, but also his closest collaborators. The latter returned to the alleged "Leninist norms of party life" precisely because the party bureaucracy could no longer tolerate Stalinist methods of intimidation and persecution. In the same vein, with all his errors, Erich Honecker was only the overseer at the top of East Germany's highly stratified, ultimately criminal Politburo. Romania's Ceausescu was altogether a different story. By appointing members of his family to top party and government positions, Ceausescu not only monopolized power, he also created a dynasty of power. The degree of hatred oppressed people feel toward their masters is bound to be quite different in the two cases.

Early deceptions

When Nicolae Ceausescu arrived at the top of Romania's Communist government in March 1965, it appeared he would de-Stalinize the Party. He condemned the holding of political prisoners, deplored the abuses of the past, and instructed the dreaded secret police, known as the *Securitate*, to abide by the law. In April 1968, he restored to honor Lucretiu Patrascanu, a former Politburo member and Marxist thinker executed in 1954 under trumped-up charges of espionage. He also reinstated into the Party many victims of his predecessor's terror. Moreover, he proclaimed the need to write a true history of both the Party and the country. He seemed to represent a kind of *glasnost* in the late 1960s, championing a self-styled version of reform communism. At the same time, the new leader de-Stalinized foreign policy. For example, he distanced Romania from the Soviet Union by vehemently condemning the Soviet invasion of Czechoslovakia in 1968.

This position won Ceausescu many points and even financial aid from Western governments. In April 1968, President Charles de Gaulle of France visited Romania and congratulated its leader for his alleged independence. In August 1969, President Richard Nixon went to Bucharest, where he was triumphantly received by an increasingly self-enamored Ceausescu. The myth of the maverick diplomat, the super-negotiator, and the only trustworthy Communist leader was accepted by Western leaders as well as the Western press, who glossed over Ceausescu's clenched fists. This image also strengthened Ceausescu by allowing him to portray dissidents as traitors, spoilers, and "wrenches in the wheel of progress."

What followed in the 1970s was a radical re-Stalinization characterized by domestic corruption and abuse. Along with the rebirth of Stalin's methods, there emerged a bizarre and unprecedented cult of personality surrounding, first, Ceausescu and then, after 1974, his wife, Elena. Several thousand people in Romania actually believed the myth that Ceausescu was the pinnacle of national dignity and sovereignty. Above all, the myth was believed by Elena, who after 1979 was second in command.

Becoming a good dictator

The only criterion for political success in Romania under Ceausescu was unconditional loyalty to the president. Ceausescu himself

General Secretary Nicolae Ceausescu before the collapse of his dictatorship. (from author's collection)

came to believe in his providential role as the "savior of the nation," the "hero of peace," and the "most brilliant revolutionary thinker of all times." He was also publicly hailed as "the Genius of the Carpathians." In an attempt to ensure his political immortality, he promoted his youngest son, Nicu, to high party positions. Ceausescu also placed his three brothers in top party positions.

Obsessed with Hitler, while believing passionately in Stalinism, Ceausescu merged these two horrifying legacies of the 20th century into a personalized tyranny. The dictator dreamed of leaving his imprint on the Romanian soul. He submitted Romanians to incredible humiliations by forcing them to pretend to be happy in times of utter poverty and despondency. He presided over the bulldozing of old Bucharest and imposed the building of a giant palace, a perfect example of "socialist realist" kitsch. Possessed by a self-image magnified to grotesque proportions by the corrupt scribes of his regime, Ceausescu completely lost touch with reality. The regime's principal engine, and only explanation for its longevity, was the *Securitate*. Like Stalin, Ceausescu managed to annihilate the Party by converting it into a passive body of almost four million members whose sole duty was to worship him.

Not only the Party, but all sources of independent social life were suppressed. In 1977, when coal workers in the Jiu Valley organized a massive strike, their leaders were captured by the *Securitate* and made to disappear. Ten years later, in November 1987, when street demonstrations took place in Brasov, the *Securitate* intervened, order was restored, and the organizers vanished. Outspoken critics were forced into either internal or external exile. There was no possibility of engaging in anything similar to Poland's Solidarity or Czechoslovakia's Charter 77. A thorough and all-pervasive police terror thwarted any attempt to launch democratic movements. Romania was almost completely paralyzed.

Under these circumstances, it is understandable that Ceausescu could not be removed as easily as the other Eastern European leaders. There was no institution that could ensure a nonviolent transition from this dictatorship to a softer version of communism. Many Romanians admitted that Ceausescu, being a tyrant, had to be removed by "tyrannicide."

The first tremors

Even before December's remarkable upheaval, 1989 was commonly seen as a disastrous year for Ceausescu's regime. His repressive political, economic, cultural, and social policies were ruining the country. Romanians were hard pressed to think of a year more miserable since the end of World War II.

The tremors of revolution began in Romania when a rare outburst of criticism occurred in early March 1989. Six former top Party and government officials sent their leader an open letter attacking his policies. The six, all former colleagues of his, accused Ceausescu of violating the 1975 Helsinki accords on human rights, which Romania had signed. He was also accused of ignoring the constitution, destroying the economy and agriculture, and indulging in what the letter writers called "hairbrained schemes" to modernize the country.

The signers included two former members of the Romanian Politburo, a foreign minister and president of the United Nations Assembly, and three veteran communists including the founder of the Romanian Party. "At a time when the very idea of socialism, for which we fought, is discredited by your policy, and when our country is being isolated from Europe, we have decided to speak up," the six wrote. "We are perfectly aware that by doing so we are risking our liberty and even our lives; but we feel duty-bound to appeal to you and reverse the present course before it is too late." Among their criticisms were the following:

The Ceausescu plan to tear down thousands of rural villages and force the removal of their inhabitants to apartment blocks.

An order forbidding all contacts between Romanian citizens and foreigners, which was used to threaten people with harassment, arrest, and loss of jobs.

The destruction and rebuilding of central Bucharest, at skyrocketing costs.

The *Securitate*'s attacks against workers demanding their rights, and against honest intellectuals exercising their right to petition.

An order forcing employees to work on Sundays.

The systematic violation of the privacy of mail and telephone services.

"To sum up, the constitution has been virtually suspended and there is no legal system in force. You must admit, Mr. President, that a society cannot function if the authorities, starting from the top, show disrespect for the law." They pointed out that economic planning no longer worked in Romania. A growing number of factories lacked raw materials, energy, or markets. "Collective agriculture is in disarray," they said, and indeed, peasants working private plots, which accounted for only 12 percent of the arable land, produced 40 percent of the vegetables, 60 percent of the milk, and 44 percent of the meat.

Romania under Ceausescu was increasingly isolated, as the signers pointed out. Several European countries closed their Bucharest embassies. Romania had lost its "most-favored-nation" status for trade with the United States, and the European Economic Community was unwilling to extend its trade agreement with Romania.

It is interesting to note that the signers were not calling for an end to Communist rule. Their letter was a mere request for "constructive dialogue that might save the system."

Ceausescu did not acknowledge the letter. A few days after copies reached the West, however, his government announced that the secret police had uncovered a "grave action of betrayal." All six signers were arrested and sent into internal exile. (Two signers, Corneliu Manescu and Silviu Brucan, both 73 years old and in failing health, nevertheless surfaced after Ceausescu's execution in December.)

Summer 1989

In July, Ceausescu played host to the annual Warsaw Pact summit conference. Reports from the conference indicated that Romania, along with East Germany and Czechoslovakia, resisted the program of *glasnost* and *perestroika* championed by Soviet leader Mikhail Gorbachev and supported by Poland and Hungary. Ceausescu also used the occasion to discuss the tense situation in western Romania. The Hungarian minority was high on Ceausescu's list of subjects that nettled him. Borders are always a fresh and serious concern in Eastern Europe. Romania lost the northern half of Moldavia to the Soviets during World War II, but it resumed its disputed possession of Transylvania, along with the Hungarian population that has historically inhabited the region. Ceausescu had problems enough enforcing loyalty among the Romanians, who hated him as a tyrant. The Hungarian minority hated him as a usurper who uprooted whole communities in his effort to reorganize rural life. The Hungarian government continued to protest Ceausescu's efforts to assimilate the millions of Hungarian residents in the region.

In August, Romania called for the Warsaw Pact to stop non-Communists from taking power in Poland. June parliamentary elections had humiliated the Polish Communist party. As Solidarity members were taking their seats in the Polish Parliament, Romanian officials complained bitterly to the Soviet Union. In November, after the fall of Erich Honecker, Ceausescu warned Romanians that nonsocialist opposition would not be tolerated.

The triggering event

The triggering event in Ceausescu's fall was the showdown in the city of Timisoara, which ended in a Tiananmen Square-style assault by the *Securitate*. Timisoara is in the Banat, the flat western frontier region where Romanians, Hungarians, Serbs, Bulgarians, Germans, and others have lived and intermarried for centuries. This intermingling has brought a sophistication and social cohesion that is rare in Romania, a country riven by mountains that isolate one ethnic group from another. Thus, in December 1989, when Communist authorities in Timisoara exiled Laszlo Tokes, a Hungarian pastor, for preaching against the regime, Romanians in Timisoara joined their fellow Hungarians in protest.

Until the Reverend Laszlo Tokes became pastor in 1986, the Reformed Church of Timisoara consisted mainly of elderly women. Tokes invigorated the membership. According to Zoltan Balaton, a member of the congregation, Tokes "gathered students and intellectuals—they were attracted by what he said and by his personality." By 1988, he had also attracted the suspicions of the *Securitate.* Anonymous callers began to threaten him; cars filled with watchful men often parked in front of the church. An architect who was working with Tokes on a church-restoration project received calls warning him to abandon the project. He refused, and in September 1989 his dead body was found in a Timisoara park. On Sundays, uniformed police, jingling their handcuffs in front of them, formed a line that members of the congregation had to pass to get to services. In November, four thugs broke into Tokes's residence, beat him, and cut his face with a knife. Finally, a court ordered an eviction, on the grounds that Tokes no longer had the right to occupy the minister's residence. The court set the eviction date for December 15. On Sunday, December 10, Tokes told his congregation what was going to happen: "If anyone would like to see an illegal eviction, I invite him to come and watch."

When the authorities arrived to remove Tokes, local Hungarians and Romanians formed a human chain to shield the pastor. Many of them were determined nonparishioners. "People were terrified," one witness reported, "but it was clear that their hatred had turned to rage." As the authorities dragged Tokes away, he shouted back to his supporters, "Do you see? Do you see?" By the following day, masses of students and workers joined the pastor's followers in the streets of Timisoara. Even the elderly, long since resigned to defeat, clamored with the students. In a matter of hours, rioting spread through the city.

The Timisoara massacre

On Sunday, December 17, in response to two days of rioting in Timisoara, Ceausescu convened a meeting of the Political Executive Committee of the Romanian Communist party. According to a transcript published some three weeks later by the newspaper *Romania Libera (Free Romania)*, there was a telecommunications hook-up from the meeting room in Bucharest to remote sites where some of his generals and security men were watching events. In the transcript, Ceausescu demanded to know why the military had yet to open fire on the demonstrators. "Why didn't they shoot?" he asked. "They should have shot to put them on the ground, to warn them—shot them in the legs." Apparently addressing his commanders on the scene, Ceausescu said, "Everybody who doesn't submit to the soldiers—I've given them the order to shoot. They'll get a warning, and if they don't submit, they'll have to be shot. It was a mistake to turn the other cheek. . . . In an hour, order should be established in Timisoara."

Ceausescu left shortly afterward for a previously planned three-day visit to Iran, probably unaware of how fragile the situation had become. His support in the Romanian army had been eroding for years. Unwisely, Ceausescu had neglected to provide adequate funds for weapons and equipment. Even more foolishly, he had reneged on the payment of some promised bonuses to the officer corps. Although there had been no meetings or conspiracies among the officers, many officers knew that they were simply unwilling to shed blood to preserve the regime.

When orders came from Bucharest after the December 17 meeting, the regime had other forces at its disposal. On the same day, thousands of people were starting a march through Timisoara. Many broke into bookstores, tore apart displays of books by and about the Ceausescus, and set them afire on the pavement. Cars were overturned, and the town hall was attacked with Molotov cocktails; some demonstrators even hurled themselves at tanks that were brought in. A large group gathered outside Communist party headquarters. The prime minister, Constantin Dascalescu, who had been sent from Bucharest to restore order, appeared on the balcony with the local Party leader, and both officials told the people to go home. The crowd booed, and cries of "Down with Ceausescu!" rang out. The officials withdrew, and the demonstrators, feeling very brave, broke into the building, tore portraits of Ceausescu from the walls, and hurled them through the windows. They broke into a storeroom and found cases of such delicacies as coffee and salami, which the Party had been hoarding. These were liberated. A fire truck came to the scene, presumably to break up the mob by spraying it with fire hoses. The crowd seized the truck and burned it. At that point, according to witnesses, armed men in civilian clothing opened fire. They were members of the *Securitate*.

The shooting spread to other quarters of the city on Sunday night. Exactly how many people died will never be known. In addition to the protesters, many army officers who refused to shoot their unarmed fellow citizens were summarily executed by the *Securitate*. There was a lot of confusion. Some witnesses said that *Securitate* agents in trucks picked up bodies and hauled them away to prevent a complete count. A month after the massacre, the new government announced that about seven hundred people were killed. The confrontation in Timisoara continued for three more days, with government forces either unable or unwilling to kill enough of the city's population to end the uprising.

Down with Ceausescu!

Ceausescu returned to Bucharest on Wednesday, December 20, and immediately addressed the nation on television. He called the Timisoara demonstrators "a few groups of hooligan elements" and scheduled a demonstration of support for the regime the next day. The Party apparatus got to work organizing a crowd and handing out the usual banners and portraits.

As the rally began on Thursday, December 21, it appeared that the regime would once again demonstrate that the people were, if not loyal, at least passive. Ceausescu, wearing a black fur hat, stepped out on to a shallow second-story balcony. Elena Ceausescu and members of the Political Executive Committee stood with him. A crowd of several thousand people had assembled. Up front, a mass of pro-government supporters cheered on cue. A few minutes into Ceausescu's speech, a lamp post wobbled and collapsed, shattering with a loud crash. A woman standing near it shrieked. Immediately, the people standing around her assumed she had been shot by the *Securitate*. Someone shouted, "Timisoara! Timisoara!" Suddenly other voices began to chant, "Rat, rat!" and "Death!" Then most people lashed out a steady chant: "Ceausescu *Dictatorul*"—Ceausescu Dictator. Some students at the edge of the crowd chose that moment to unfurl a homemade banner they had been secretly carrying: "DOWN WITH CEAUSESCU." Other people began to flee.

A demonstrator carries the Romanian flag with the
Communist symbol cut out, joining thousands at an anti-
Ceausescu rally. (AP/Wide World Photos)

The noise and confusion seemed to startle Ceausescu. A look
of stricken surprise lingered on his face. According to witnesses,
he stopped speaking and waved his arms. "What? No, no . . . Hello,
hello," he said, apparently thinking that something was wrong with
the microphone. For a moment, he looked old, bewildered, and
vulnerable. Elena Ceausescu stepped up to the microphone and
called for silence. The confusion lasted for three minutes, during
which Romanian television interrupted the broadcast and played
patriotic music. Propelled by a sharp jab from his wife, Ceausescu

continued his speech, but the damage had been done. The shrieks and confusion, the chanting, combined with the interruption of the broadcast, had produced a moment of weakness. It was the end of Ceausescu. That single episode destroyed forever the notion that he was invulnerable. And the people had finally heard their own voices.

The dictator's downfall came the next morning. He made a final effort to speak to angry crowds from the balcony of the Central Committee building. The people booed and threw potatoes and shoes at him. He retreated inside the building and again ordered the army to fire on the crowds. Later that morning, the minister of defense was shot; his death was announced as a traitor's suicide. Later, the military explained that the minister had shot himself rather than carry out his orders. Many people believed, however, that Ceausescu had ordered the minister's summary execution. However it occurred, the minister's death did not bend the army to Ceausescu's will. By that time, most of the troops were joining the crowds in the streets. One crowd surged against the Central Committee building and began to break in. Mortified, Ceausescu and his wife climbed the stairs to the landing pad on the roof. They squeezed into a helicopter and fled the city.

A brief and bloody civil war

Ceausescu had left behind his security forces with orders to sow as much chaos as possible. Numbering as many as 15,000, they disappeared into the narrow, ancient streets of Bucharest, Timisoara, Constanta, Brasov, and Cluj. These were the cities that turned into fierce battle zones for several days. The *Securitate* perched themselves in safe houses and tunnels equipped for long-term survival. Gathering courage, they commandeered cars, trucks, and helicopters to terrorize the population. Skilled snipers murdered countless victims with a single shot to the head. Some victims were dragged away to be tortured.

Most of the country's 23 million citizens watched the chaos on television. On the day Ceausescu fell, the army captured the television station and began to broadcast the fighting throughout the country. When *Securitate* fighters tried to seize the station, the army dug in. After midnight, shells slammed into the 13-story building, and bullets shattered its windows. Troops inside replied with a withering barrage. None of the defenders had fired more than a handful of rounds in their lives—and never at anything that shot back.

After the terrifying siege, the first screen images of Free Romanian Television flickered, broadcasting an appeal for help. Within minutes, more than three thousand people flooded the square in front of the station and formed a human shield between the station and the *Securitate* positions. As news was broadcast, the *Securitate* withdrew. But Romanians were riveted by reports that as many as sixty thousand people had been killed in other pitched battles between the army and the *Securitate*. They were told that they were unique in Eastern Europe: Their Stalinist dictator could be toppled only at great human cost.

Stories of the *Securitate*'s cunning and brutality dominated the broadcasts. In Timisoara's Opera Square, as bells and horns sounded to honor the thousands who had fallen only days earlier, the security forces fired into the crowd of more than one hundred thousand people. More than 160 people were killed. The next day, more crowds gathered and the shooting continued. One witness said that the *Securitate*'s forces were even shooting at ambulances as they attempted to evacuate the wounded.

Horror stories continued. The body of a pregnant woman was discovered in a pile of corpses. Her belly had been ripped open, and her legs were wound tightly with barbed wire. Parents searched through open graves for the bodies of their missing children. Hands were missing, tongues were cut out. No one could understand the brutality of the *Securitate*. An employee at a small hospital described how "Ceausescu's henchmen" went to the hospitals after the first bloodletting on December 17 and collected many of the wounded. They were taken to the morgue, tortured, and killed. Other witnesses explained how some security forces mingled with the regular army soldiers. "Then they would shoot the soldiers in the back of the head and disappear like snakes."

In Bucharest an army tank fights with the *Securitate* and other pro-Ceausescu forces on December 23. Romanian citizens take cover behind the tank. (Reuters/Bettmann Archives)

Christmas Day 1989

Where was the dictator? Was he managing the *Securitate* from some remote underground bunker? Had he fled into the Soviet Union? As skirmishes and full-fledged battles erupted throughout Romania, Ceausescu seemed omnipresent. As it turned out, Ceausescu's helicopter had landed near Tirgoviste, a city northwest of Bucharest. His wicked entourage had commandeered a car, driven to a nearby town, and hidden in a seed-distribution center. The local police found them, however, and handed them over to the army, which kept them in an armored car for three days.

On Christmas Day, in a barracks about 50 miles outside of Bucharest, the "Epoch of Light" was drawing to a rapid close. For two hours, a military tribunal tried the Ceausescus. They were charged with "serious crimes against the people, which are incompatible with human dignity." In answer to charges of genocide and subversion of the national economy, the couple defiantly challenged the right of their accusers to judge them.

Ceausescu (*arguing loudly*): I do not recognize this court. Read the constitution.

Ousted dictator Ceausescu with his wife, Elena, at their televised interview during their trial on Christmas Day. They were executed only minutes later. (AP/Wide World Photo)

Prosecutor: We have read the constitution. We know it better than you do.

Ceausescu: I will not answer a single question.

Prosecutor: What possessed you to reduce the people to the state they were in? Why did the people have to starve?

Ceausescu: This is a lie that proves the lack of patriotism in the country. . . .

Prosecutor: What have you done for the country?

Ceausescu: I built hospitals.

Prosecutor: You destroyed the Romanian people and their economy.

Ceausescu: We do not intend to argue with you. The population had everything it needed. . . .

Prosecutor: Who ordered the shooting of the people?

Ceausescu (*staring at the ceiling*): I will not answer a single question. Do not interpret my silence as answers. I will answer only to the working class.

Prosecutor: There are more than 64,000 dead in the cities.

Elena (*angrily*): This is a provocation!

Prosecutor: All you did was science?

Elena (*shouting*): I am president of the Romanian Academy of Sciences! I am the first Deputy Prime Minister.

Prosecutor: Let Ceausescu tell us something about his Swiss bank accounts.

Elena: Evidence, evidence, evidence!

Ceausescu: There is not a single account. You are a provocateur. . . .

Prosecutor (*reading the verdict*): On the basis of the actions of the members of the Ceausescu family, we condemn the two of you to death.

Ceausescu (*defiantly*): I am not a defendant. I am President of Romania and the Commander in Chief of the armed forces. I refuse to recognize this court.

A *voice interrupts, ordering the pair to rise.*

Elena (*to her husband*): No, dear, we will not rise.

There was an abundance of volunteers to serve on the firing squad. When the squad formed, the Ceausescus were reported to have run wildly around the courtyard of the barracks where they were tried. The dictator was finally trapped in a corner and shot, while Elena Ceausescu kept running. She was ultimately shot in the back with a pistol by an army officer.

Late the next night, Free Romanian Television showed Ceausescu lying on his back by a battered brick wall, his eyes staring, a pool of blood near his head. The camera lingered over his body for nearly a minute. Romanians let out a collective sigh of relief at the visible proof that change was possible.

The Front for National Salvation

When the new provisional leaders, calling themselves the Front for National Salvation (NSF), appeared in a broadcast on Free Romanian Television on December 23, the people were euphoric. After Ceausescu's execution, the Front worked quickly to reverse some of the dictator's worst excesses. In doing so, they returned Romania to the 20th century. They turned on the heat and hot water in freezing apartments; they loaded shop shelves with warehoused food intended for export; they made precious imported goods—such as coffee, chocolate, and oranges, which had previously been reserved for Party officials and members of the *Securitate*—available to the starving public. During the first weeks after Ceausescu's execution, the Front also abolished the death penalty, released political prisoners, and issued passports.

The NSF quickly reassured both East and West that Romania's "traditional role in the center of Europe" would be reasserted. The interim leaders' first official statement promised both "to observe commitments with the Warsaw Pact" and "to direct the entire foreign policy to united Europe." Simultaneously, it was announced that Romania would terminate the Communist party's leading role.

For many Romanians, these later measures were not enough. Unlike several of their Eastern European neighbors, Romania did not formally dissolve or immediately reconstitute its Communist party, which reportedly had more than four million members. Moreover, the presence of former Party officials in the interim government sparked a series of protests. But Romanians were discovering a taste for politics. For the first time in 45 years, people could speak openly about their worries, criticize the new leaders, and organize independent political associations and political parties.

Change?

Was communism finished in Romania? Did the revolution and Ceausescu's execution usher in full-fledged democracy? Had lives been lost for nothing? The members of the Front who organized his execution were themselves former communists. It is unclear why the NSF leaders organized Ceausescu's trial in a manner disturbingly similar to Stalin's frame-ups. Furthermore, there were indications that former leaders of the *Securitate* were among the first to lend their support to the new authorities.

How can one stop a spontaneous revolution among civilian masses from being influenced by those adept in the totalitarian techniques of manipulation? Many Romanians think this is what happened. What else can explain the tremendous force of the revolution and yet its failure to create political forms that would guarantee a break with the past?

In its first statement, the Front announced a commitment to democratic principles—including a multi-party system—and the need to organize free elections as soon as possible. The Front claimed to represent a decisive break with the abhorred Communist regime. Next, the Romanian Communist party disappeared without trace from the country's political life. But Romania's Communist party had long ago lost all autonomy. It had become an appendage of the Ceausescu dynasty, a huge machine whose sole duty was to extol the president and his wife.

At their trial, Nicolae and Elena Ceausescu challenged their judges and accused Romania's new leaders of treason and attempting a putsch. Because the basic legal procedures were ignored, many observers saw the trial as a judicial murder. Others, of course, thought the execution was not brutal enough. The Front, however, justified the summary execution by invoking reasons of "revolutionary expediency." Many Romanians doubted this explanation and suspected that the sham trial served to eliminate the dictator and his wife as potentially embarrassing witnesses in an inevitable trial of the Romanian Communist party.

New leaders

The composition of the new leadership was rather striking. The Council of the NSF was led by a foursome of old communists. Its chairman, 60-year-old Ion Iliescu, studied in Moscow in the early 1950s and was Ceausescu's protege until 1971, when he fell in disgrace for "intellectualism." Presumably anti-Stalinist, he is far from being anti-Communist. His model is Gorbachev, and his ideal is a reformed version of the one-party system. Since his rise to power, Iliescu has not kept these convictions secret. On the contrary, in a debate with student leaders on January 21, 1990, Iliescu described political pluralism as "an obsolete ideology of the nineteenth century." In his speech, which was not published in the still state-controlled Romanian media but publicized by the Soviet press agency TASS, Iliescu claimed that the NSF advocated a "democratic model without pluralism." In this, he was echoing not only Gorbachev's opposition to a multi-party system, but also the political philosophy of the NSF's principal thinker, communist veteran Silviu Brucan.

Born in 1916, Silviu Brucan could take advantage of his dissident past. He was one of the authors of the "Letter of Six," the political indictment of the Ceausescu regime. With surprising candor, however, Brucan has expressed his deep contempt for Western-type democracy. His is the concept that, because the recent Romanian revolution is so original, its aftermath must essentially be different from those of other countries. For Brucan, as for Iliescu, terms like socialism, communism, capitalism, and fascism have lost any sense. They consider the NSF to be a mass party movement. In the light of this outlook, there is no need for other political parties to exist and compete for power with the "truly national exponent," that is, the Front for National Salvation.

The new prime minister and third member of the quartet, Petre Roman, was born in 1946. Roman's only revolutionary credentials were that he had participated in the December 22 storming of the Central Committee building along with thousands of other Romanians. Fluent in French and Spanish, holding a degree from a French university, Roman was supposed to provide the new leadership with a badly needed European and youthful veneer. Roman, however, had never raised his voice as one with Romania's oppressed. Many people felt Roman's foreign credentials clashed with the genuine revolutionary fervor in the streets.

The fourth member of the initial ruling quartet, Dumitru Mazilu, resigned on January 26, 1990, in protest against the "Stalinist methods of the new leadership." Mazilu knows something about Stalinism: A former *Securitate* colonel, he taught international law at the University of Bucharest and served as the government-appointed United Nations expert on human rights. In 1987, he smuggled out of Romania his report on human rights violations in the country.

Many Romanians were deeply troubled by the conflict between the Front and Mazilu. Was it a simple clash of ambitions? Or were they witnessing an obscure struggle between two groups that had secretly conspired to take over power? After Mazilu's resignation, the leadership of the NSF remained in the hands of the Iliescu-Brucan-Roman triad. To counter charges of a Communist plot inside the NSF to take control, the Front decided to include in the larger Council a number of well-known oppositional figures. Among them were human rights activist Doina Cornea, writer Aurel Dragos Munteanu, and poets Ana Blandiana, Dan Desliu, and Mircea Dinescu. Each was associated with a desire for vigorous change. Finally, the Front announced that free elections would be held in May 1990.

New political parties

Learning the democratic process is difficult in a country with very few democratic traditions. The unique political education of the Romanians continued as new political parties were formed. Many of the parties had existed in Romania's fragile pre-World War II democracy, such as the Peasant party, the Liberal party, and the Social Democrats. As many as 50 additional groups emerged over the first difficult months as Romania headed toward free elections. For the time being, the Communist party kept a low profile and did not try to reestablish itself. Many of the Communists' activists, however, tried to emulate the Hungarian strategy, for example, proposing the formation of a "Socialist party." All in all, it seemed that in a matter of weeks Romania had made an extraordinary leap from the political numbness of one era to the frenzy and color of another.

But the Front for National Salvation dominated the activities. Was it possible to support the Front and still hold membership in one of the newly created political parties? In fact, the major source of instability in Romania after Ceausescu seems to have been born out of the ambitions of the Front. The Front maintained that it represented a provisional form of government and that its only mission was to create a peaceful transition to pluralism. But on January 29, the Front organized a massive demonstration against the opposition parties. The Front's supporters shouted slogans that charged the opposition with the aim of destabilizing the country's political life.

Then, in February, the Front threw off its disguise and became a political party. From that moment on, it started to lose credibility among the masses of students and intellectuals. One of the country's most influential columnists, Octavian Paler, wrote in the independent newspaper *Romania Libera* that the Front was opportunistic. He accused the NSF of taking advantage of its revolutionary image in order to neutralize the opposition and ensure its own victory in the election. Moreover, Paler wrote, the Front was relinquishing its aura as the "good witch of the revolutionary spontaneity" of December 1989.

Following the Front's decision to become a party, political forces polarized. On the one hand, there was the Front, whose political options are often described as neo-communist; on the other, there were the opposition parties, dominated by the Peasants, Liberals, and Social Democrats. The NSF also created a number of satellite parties ready to endorse the Front's platform in the hope of sharing power. To make matters more confusing—and disappointing—Iliescu relied on the time-tested practices of his predecessor: He used force to break up peaceful rallies calling for more democracy. In addition, Romanians knew that the dreaded *Securitate* had not been dismantled. Instead of purging the administrative apparatus of the old regime, the NSF appointed many of its members to key positions.

The Timisoara Proclamation

A mass rally in Timisoara's Opera Square on March 11, 1990, became an important turning point in Romania's struggle for freedom. More than fifteen thousand people gathered, and the Timisoara Proclamation was read.

The Proclamation articulated with tremendous clarity the expectations and values of those who started the revolution. Almost at once, the document became the rallying point for all democratic forces in Romania. It was endorsed by hundreds of groups and associations. Article 1 of the Proclamation stated that the revolution was, "from the beginning, not only anti-Ceausescu but also explicitly anti-communist. . . . In keeping with the aspirations of millions of people in Eastern Europe, we demand the immediate abolition of this totalitarian and bankrupt system. The ideal of the revolution was and remains a return to the genuine values of democracy and European civilization."

Article 8 of the Proclamation was equally resonant. It called for the modification of electoral law in order to prevent former members of the *Securitate* from holding government jobs or running for parliamentary seats. With greater fierceness, the document opposed the right of those who had served in the Communist regime to stand for the office of president. The Proclamation hit its target.

The offended officials reacted predictably. The Front-controlled newspapers and Romanian television tried to dismiss the relevance of the Proclamation. It was called unrealistic, absurd, and disruptive. But for the many Romanians who had fought in the streets, the Timisoara Proclamation became the charter of Romania's emancipation from communism.

On April 22, several thousand people—students, teachers, professionals, and workers—seized University Square in Bucharest, where they briefly blocked traffic on the busy intersections. About fifty of the demonstrators proceeded to organize a sit-in protesting the government's refusal to accept the Timisoara Proclamation. Two days later, Iliescu unleashed hundreds of riot police in a pre-dawn raid. The reaction to the raid, and to the six hundred armed police left behind on guard, brought thousands of people to the square. Shouting "Collaborators!" and "You shot at us in December!" the furious crowd herded the police out of the square, and more and more demonstrators flooded in. Confronted with this unwavering challenge, Iliescu was so angry that he called the protesters *golani*, or "tramps." This sort of name-calling was hauntingly reminiscent of Ceausescu's outburts against the "hooligans" of Timisoara during the first days of revolution. In a matter of hours, thousands of Romanians were giggling and calling themselves "golani" to show their support for the demonstrators.

Free elections—May 20, 1990

Despite these victories, the results of the elections were disappointing for the revolutionaries. Apparently, the resonance of the Timisoara Proclamation fell on many deaf ears. Its supporters wondered how it happened that the country, which broke so dramatically with its old regime, should install a new government filled with old Communists.

The election took place on May 20, 1990, as scheduled. Ion Iliescu was elected president with a landslide of 80 percent of the vote. He clearly had the support of his people. The 16 million electorate, which turned out in its entirety, knew that he and nearly all his aids in the Front had been Communists who worked for Ceausescu. The voters also were aware that thousands viewed the Front with suspicion, even hatred.

Part of the explanation lies, of course, with the gross inequalities of the electoral campaign. The opposition newspapers, so freely available at Bucharest hotels open only to wealthy Party members and Western tourists, had been unavailable in many parts of the country. Television, a more powerful medium than print in the countryside, remained firmly under Front control; time was allocated fairly to the parties for election broadcasts, but the news bulletins and discussion programs were slanted toward the Front. And the most powerful mass medium of all—rumor—worked overtime against the opposition parties. Rumor had it that Ion Ratiu, the emigre millionare who became the Peasant's presidential candidate, was planning to either buy the whole country or sell it. Rumor had it that Doina Cornea, the human rights activist, was Ratiu's mistress, and that her daughter was planning to buy the Romanian steel industry. Rumor even had it that Ratiu, who comes from a famous political family that fought against Hungarian rule in Transylvania, was really a Hungarian called Jonas Rac.

But the most important rumors, which may have gained millions of votes for the Front, concerned jobs and money. The workers on collective farms were told that they would lose their pension rights if the land were redistributed. They were told that their elderly parents would therefore become destitute overnight. The factory workers were told that if capitalists were let into Romania they would buy the factories and close them down.

Perhaps the most valid reasons for the Front's victory do not lie just in the campaign. They lie in the previous 42 years. A whole population had been brutalized, poorly educated even by Communist standards, and starved of information about the real world. Interestingly, the stronghold of support for the Front is the northeastern province of Moldavia—geographically the furthest away from the West, insulated by distance from the Western tourism of Bucharest. Everything that was miserable and oppressive about the Romanian system, the Moldavians blamed on Ceausescu, not on communism.

The future of democracy

There is a Danubian parable that eerily evokes Romania today. A young hero lops off the head of an evil dragon, only to see that the blood that gurgles out of the dragon's neck spreads pestilence throughout the countryside for years.

The fall of Nicolae Ceausescu in December 1989 marked the end of four decades of Communist tyranny. It was an extremely

Anti-government demonstrators in Bucharest in June 1990.
(AP/Wide World Photos)

expensive (in human lives) but welcome Christmas present. Romania's revolution, however, is unfinished. Ever since its initial May
elections, Bucharest has been the scene of bloodshed. As in Bulgaria, Albania, and the southern two-thirds of Yugoslavia, the Communist party still desperately hangs on to power—even if, as in
Romania, it has been freely elected under a new name. Romania

is not a country in which the Communists suppressed a democratic tradition; Romania never had a democratic tradition. The Communist system will not be buried in Romania until greater numbers of people recognize Stalin's face in the Front's leadership. Washing away the dragon's blood may take years.

6 SOVIET UNION

An Empire Crumbles

Tens of thousands of Azerbaijani nationalists defy Moscow's warnings and gather under the shadow of Lenin on Baku's main square on September 9, 1989. Moments later, Gorbachev announced sweeping reforms in the Soviet federal system. (Reuters/Bettmann Archives)

A CHRONOLOGY OF EVENTS IN THE SOVIET UNION

October 1917	The October Revolution; Vladimir Lenin establishes a Communist government.
1922	Joseph Stalin becomes general secretary of the Communist party.
February 1945	At Yalta, the Allies agree to allow the Soviets to retain positions in Eastern Europe.
March 5, 1953	Stalin dies; Nikita Khrushchev succeeds him.
May 14, 1955	The Warsaw Pact is formed.
October 1964	Khrushchev is ousted and replaced as general secretary by Leonid Brezhnev.
March 11, 1985	Mikhail Gorbachev is named as general secretary.
March 17, 1986	The Communist party approves "truly revolutionary changes" in the economy.
February 26, 1988	More than seven hundred thousand people protest in Azerbaijan and Armenia.
March 1989	In the first free elections since 1917, scores of Party officials suffer humiliating defeats.
April 1, 1989	Soviet troops begin to withdraw from Hungary, Czechoslovakia, and East Germany.

January 13, 1990	Violent ethnic clashes break out in Azerbaijan.
February 4, 1990	One hundred thousand people demonstrate against the Communist party in Moscow.
February 7, 1990	Article Six of the Soviet Constitution is eliminated.
February 24, 1990	The Communists are defeated in Lithuanian elections.
March 18, 1990	Latvia and Estonia favor independence from the Soviet Union; Gorbachev is elected by the Soviet Parliament to a new executive presidency.
April 13, 1990	Gorbachev announces economic blockade of Lithuania.
May 4, 1990	The Latvian Parliament votes for independence, but with an indeterminate transition period.
July 2, 1990	Boris Yeltsin, leader of the Russian republic and Gorbachev's chief rival, quits the Communist party.
November 17, 1990	Gorbachev announces that executive power will be wielded by himself and the presidents of the 15 republics.

GIVEN THE CASCADE of events and emotions that occurred in Eastern Europe in the fall of 1989, it was tempting to predict the future, based on the logic of the immediate past. The extraordinary revolutions and democratic movements in Eastern Europe unfolded under the gaze, with the approval, and sometimes, incredibly, at the prodding of the Soviet government under the leadership of Mikhail Gorbachev. Not least among the astounding aspects of Gorbachev's policy was the apparent equanimity with which he accepted the fall of communism in the Soviet satellite countries. The big question was: Would the Soviet Union be next?

The Communist party

"The Soviet socialist experiment has been the great utopian adventure of our century," one scholar wrote about the Soviet Union. "For more than 70 years, to millions it has meant hope, and to other millions, horror; but for all it has spelled fascination." Vladimir Lenin was the founder of the Union of Soviet Socialist Republics (Soviet Union). In 1917, Lenin galvanized a revolutionary movement that toppled centuries of imperial rule and created the world's first Communist nation. The new leader established a socialist government that was based on the ideas of Karl Marx, a 19th-century political philosopher. In simplest terms, socialism is a system of government in which land and industry are controlled by the government rather than by individuals or private companies. Borrowing Marx's socialist teachings, Lenin created a framework that was both socialist and authoritartian. To ensure the success of his economic program, Lenin eliminated all political parties and opposition groups in the new nation. He made sure that the Communist party retained all power.

Lenin dominated the Communist party by virtue of his experience, intellect, and strong will. Although other leaders did not hesitate to disagree with him, he was widely admired and respected. In the early 1920s, Lenin began to rely on Joseph Stalin, who became general secretary, or chief administrator, of the Party in 1922. *Stalin*, or "steel," was a revolutionary pseudonym. His real name was Dzhugashvili. Stalin rose in the ranks of the Party by determination, hard work, and thoroughness. As early as 1921, when he helped arrange the forcible incorporation of his native Georgia into the new Union of Soviet Socialist Republics, Stalin showed he could be ruthless and decisive. Partly because of Stalin's methods and attitudes, Lenin became increasingly critical of him in 1922 and 1923.

After Lenin's death in 1924, Stalin won a power struggle to succeed Lenin as undisputed leader of the Party and dictator of the Soviet Union. For the next 30 years, the Soviet Union endured some of the most brutal repression in modern history. Later on, under Nikita Khrushchev and Leonid Brezhnev, the genocide and bloody atrocities ended, but the Communist party remained in control of all the centers of power. The Party was the steering apparatus, and together with its bureaucracy, its presence could be clearly felt not only in the police and the army but also in the economy. The Communist party was identified with the state, and no one would have dreamed of protesting. According to many Soviet historians, its iron grip was necessary to hold together the various republics and the more than one hundred national groups within the Soviet Union. (Eventually, all the nations that fell into Stalin's sphere of influence after World War II adopted this tyrannical system, voluntarily or under duress.)

The rise of Gorbachev

In March 1985, Mikhail Gorbachev was chosen to succeed Konstantin Chernenko as general secretary of the Soviet Communist party. In his mid-fifties, Gorbachev possessed a dynamic and assertive style of leadership. In summer 1985, for example, a typical story about Gorbachev was circulating in Moscow. The new general secretary took an utterly inconceivable step: He decided to go for a walk and talk to the "man in the street" in a relaxed and informal way. He first turned up unannounced in Moscow suburbs to address workers in factories and cafeterias. Later, during a visit to Leningrad, he strolled unescorted along the crowded boulevards, with the Soviet media close on his heels. Yet, that evening, when Gorbachev watched the news, there was no mention of his stroll through the Leningrad streets. It turned out that all appearances of the Party secretary had to follow strict Party guidelines; Gorbachev's conduct was so unusual that the Kremlin had to apply vigorous pressure to get the media accustomed to airing such practices.

No one had ever had to *think* about the correct media presentation of the top hierarchy. Neither Brezhnev nor Stalin had behaved even remotely like Gorbachev. Stalin, the "Old Master," had seldom spoken on the radio, nor had he appeared on television (which was still in its infancy when he died in 1953). In addition, it was intrinsic to the system, even when the tsar was in power, that the ruler have an unapproachable aura and be glimpsed only from a distance. Brezhnev was uncomfortable speaking in public and followed the tradition of Russia's pre-revolutionary royalty.

As a result, the open, uncomplicated manner of Gorbachev was regarded as new and sensational. The media representatives, the officials, and certainly the public were completely bewildered. "Centuries of tsarism and then 70 years of Soviet rule," one scholar explained, "had been brutally and violently forced on the people, creating an almost slavish obeisance." On the other hand, this absolute allegiance and servility had produced a feeling of safety and security. But now Gorbachev was calling on the Soviets to throw off their fears and traditional submissiveness and to take charge of their lives. This challenge was novel and perplexing; it would take a long time to comprehend it.

At his first Warsaw Pact meeting as General Secretary of the Soviet Communist party, Mikhail Gorbachev signs new trade agreements with the Polish delegation. (CAF/Warszawa)

Perestroika

By his own admission, Gorbachev inherited an enormous backlog of problems. Domestically, the Soviet Union was in economic, political, and moral decline. Expenditures on the Soviet arms buildup had long exceeded the country's capability to pay for them and at the same time maintain the population's standard of living. Externally, the country faced numerous challenges, ranging from the collapse of relations with the West to the stalemate in the war against the Afghan resistance.

From the very outset, Gorbachev made it clear that his first priority was to invigorate the stagnant economy, and he spoke of the need to "restructure the economic mechanism." On assuming office, Gorbachev and his associates expected to have a fairly easy time reviving the economy. In Gorbachev's own words: "We had initially assumed that basically the task was only to correct certain deformations of the social organs, to perfect the entire system set in place during the preceding decades." The premise turned out to be wrong. By the end of 1985, Gorbachev had concluded that "everything pertaining to the economy, culture, democracy, foreign policy—all spheres—had to be reappraised."

The reappraisal was harsh. Not only was the economy stagnant or even contracting, there was, Gorbachev wrote, an erosion of moral values. Propaganda about Soviet accomplishments, real or imagined, had crowded out real discussion of the country's problems. Science, the arts, journalism, and culture had been "emasculated." Corruption was common among officials, as was disrespect for the law, "servility, opportunism, and glorification," and the "mass distribution of awards." "Social justice" was often violated. The country, in short, was ripe for change.

Once Gorbachev realized the immensity of the Soviet Union's economic problems, he dropped the original slogan *uskorenie*, or "acceleration," for *perestroika*, or "restructuring." The latter entailed reducing the grip of the bureaucracy on the country as well as stimulating the private initiative in all spheres of national life. Essentially, it meant bringing society into a limited partnership with the ruling elite, making it an active participant in the life of the country.

Glasnost

From the beginning, Gorbachev understood that his effort to restructure the Soviet economy would encounter at least two obstacles: the resistance of the Party bureaucracy and the passivity of the people. In order to diminish these obstacles to economic growth, he decided to introduce *glasnost*. Greater freedom of speech was intended to expose the misdeeds of "Brezhnevite" bureaucracy and thereby mobilize the support of the people.

Nothing has won Gorbachev greater admiration in the West than the policy of *glasnost,* or openness. One writer described *glasnost* as "the loosening of censorship designed to propagate images that are totally at variance with reality no less than with the private opinions of the Soviet citizens." (In truth, censorship was loosened, not abolished, since its organ, *Glavit,* continued to operate.) By the end of 1985, it began to look as if Soviet writers were being given the opportunity to be more candid. Initially, though, the new candor was applied very selectively as a means of exposing and weeding out corruption in society. There was no mention in the Soviet press, for example, of the anti-Soviet protests and clashes between Latvian and Russian youths in Riga in May that were reported in Western newspapers.

Gorbachev's policy of openness caught the world by surprise. The Soviet regime had been assuring its citizens for decades that they lived in the most progressive and prosperous country in the world. If that were the case, why change? To justify *perestroika,* it was necessary to tell the truth about the country's desperate conditions. Apparently the Communist leaders, victimized by their own propaganda, believed it would be enough to blame the country's ills on Stalin and Brezhnev. However, freedom of opinion, once unleashed, was difficult to keep up with. "It kept probing the limits of the permissible," one Soviet said. Thus, questioning the past inevitably led to questioning the present. A Soviet scholar explained: "Every exposure of a lie, every breaking of a taboo, opened a breach in the fortress of official mythology through which poured critics ready to assault the next bastion." The censors, confused by vague instructions, lost their bearings.

The limits of free speech were constantly being tested. On the whole, Lenin was still beyond the pale of criticism, although on some occasions he was attacked for instituting concentration camps. It was also revealed that Lenin gave the order to murder the tsar and his family. But the Hitler-Stalin pact, the Soviet massacre of Polish officers in the Katyn forest, and the corruption of Party officials were all favorite topics in the transforming Soviet media. So was the true condition of Soviet society. Criticizing the current leadership, however, was not tolerated.

Taking advantage of the new openness, hundreds of independent publications emerged. They ranged from gossip-filled magazines to complex academic journals. The majority of them were pro-democracy and pro-Western. Nonetheless, there was something very strange about the coexistence of a relatively free press alongside a one-party regime. Many Soviets complained that the new openness was not enough. A Russian writer explained that *glasnost* contributed to the feeling that the reforms were "not likely to last and would end in either full freedom or no freedom."

The nationalism question

In early 1989, Mikhail Gorbachev declared the nationality question to be one of the most urgent and dangerous issues facing the Soviet Union. The so-called "nationality question" was what is elsewhere known as imperialism or colonialism. Unlike the United States, whose multinational population consists overwhelmingly of immigrants who voluntarily left their native lands, the Soviet Union owes its ethnic diversity to conquests. It is the last empire in the world. While helping to liberate the subject people of foreign powers, it has insisted on maintaining intact its own empire, which it inherited from the tsars.

The growth of the Russian empire began in the middle of the 16th century. Russia expanded relentlessly along its frontiers, destroying and annexing one nation after another. By 1900, Russians made up only 44 percent of the empire's population. Today, they are only 52 percent, but because of a low birthrate they may be a minority soon.

Because their expansion occurred in neighboring lands rather than overseas, Russians were never conscious of building a colonial empire. They treated the conquered peoples as ethnic minorities who they expected, sooner or later, to give in to Russia's superior political and economic might and to assimilate. They were sure that the aspirations of the non-Russian peoples would be fully satisfied by Russian (or Soviet) occupation.

This was also Lenin's personal view. But eager to gain the support of ethnic groups in his drive for power, he promised each of them the right to full self-government up to and including secession. He did not believe they would exercise this right, but if they did, he could always force them back into the fold by exercising the superior right of "proletarian self-determination," by which he meant the interest of his Party. After the Russian Revolution, the Soviet Union built a loose federation in which the major ethnic groups could enjoy certain symbolic rights of statehood, but authority resided in the hands of a single Communist party completely dominated by Russians.

As a result of *glasnost*, people began to protest the government openly in the streets. (Reuters/Bettmann Archives)

The expectation that non-Russians would assimilate proved wrong. In fact, many historians think that the ethnic groups are more aware of their national identities today than they were before the Russian Revolution. As soon as Gorbachev's *glasnost* permitted their expression, smoldering ethnic tensions and frustrations rose to the surface. In all the republics, there are now native "fronts," or opposition groups, agitating for national rights. What do these people want? The answer differs from region to region, and depends largely on a given group's cultural and economic level of development, as well as its relations with its neighbors.

The empire begins to crumble

Glasnost succeeded in bringing about a social awakening, but not the kind Gorbachev had in mind. It developed on the Soviet fringe rather than in the heart of Russia. It fed the desire for freedom, not the spirit of submission and obedience. Between 1988 and 1990, Armenians fought with Azerbaijanis over territory; anti-Russian riots took place in Kazakhstan; Crimean Tatars, who were deported by Stalin to Central Asia, demonstrated in Moscow for the right to return home; and the people of the Baltic republics challenged the very foundation of their ties to the Soviet Union. From Central Asia to Europe, the Soviet empire was crumbling. After four years in power, Gorbachev discovered that the reform of the Soviet system and the stability of the Soviet empire were incompatible.

Gorbachev's first nationalist headache originated in Transcaucasia, the land bridge located between the Black Sea and the Caspian Sea. In February 1988, ethnic violence occurred in Armenia and Azerbaijan, two neighboring Transcaucasian republics. Although the Armenians now seek the preservation of their culture and language in the face of Russian influences, originally Armenian nationalism was not separatist, or even anti-Soviet. Its strength came from the memory of the the 1915 massacre of 1.5 million Armenians by the Turks. The Armenian campaign to reclaim the Nagornyi Karabakh province inside Azerbaijan was less directed at Moscow than at Azerbaijan, which has a Turkish population. On paper the claim was a rational one: to reunite a territory populated mainly by Armenians with the rest of Armenia.

On February 26, 1988, the republics of Armenia and Azerbaijan were paralysed by strikes. According to many reports, crowds of seven hundred thousand to one million people gathered in the capital cities. Gorbachev appeared on television, appealing to the people of both republics for calm and a "reasonable approach" to the Nagornyi Karabakh issue based on the "Leninist principles of nationalities policy." He complained that the Armenians and Azerbaijanis were "stabbing *perestroika* in the back."

Some reports noted that, after Gorbachev's televised speech, many Armenian protesters began to carry portraits of the Soviet leader. Evidently, they were prepared to put their faith in Gorbachev and *perestroika*. "This is the first time in 67 years," one Armenian said, "that Moscow has set eyes on us." On February 27, the same Armenian told a huge group of protesters: "Why are we here today? Because at last someone has allowed us to raise our heads, to come down into the streets and to speak out." By the end of March, however, as many as 50 Armenians and Azerbaijanis were dead.

Baltic nationalism

The rise of nationalism in the three Baltic republics was more overtly political. The most important thing about the Baltic opposition movements was that they challenged the very basis of Moscow's right to govern. The issue in the Baltics was the forced annexation of Estonia, Latvia, and Lithuania in 1940 and the subsequent imprisonments and executions of their leaders. Until they were swallowed by the Soviet Union, these nations were independent, sovereign states.

Before Gorbachev-era reforms were introduced, the subject of Stalin's forced annexation of the Baltics was taboo. But in the fall of 1988, commemoration of the annexation became an occasion for national self-assertion. Stretching *glasnost* to the utmost, Lithuania printed the secret protocols of the Hitler-Stalin pact of 1939. Balts could read for the first time how the Soviet Union and Germany had agreed to take over their governments and end their sovereignty. As a result, the denunciation of Stalinist crimes—a favorite theme of *glasnost*—led to the debunking of the official Soviet myth about the "voluntary union" of 1940, and thus to questions about the very legitimacy of Soviet rule.

Since the Balts were the last to "join" the Soviet Union, it seemed only natural that they would be the most sensitive to the constraints on their autonomy. In late 1988, two proposed amendments to the Soviet Constitution also stirred political nationalism. The first amendment strengthened the right of the Supreme Soviet in Moscow to overrule decisions by the parliaments in individual republics. The second amendment gave the Soviets the right to declare martial law and other "special forms of administration." The first was rejected by the Balts as negating the "right to secession" ostensibly recognized by the Soviet Constitution. The "special powers" amendment, although introduced with the Armenian conflict in mind, was also taken personally by the Balts, who feared it could apply to them.

More than 10,000 Estonians at the nationalist rally in Tallinn Park in August 1989 commemorating the 50th anniversary of the Hitler-Stalin pact. (Reuters/Bettmann Archives)

The Communist party's insensitivity in pushing through the amendments bolstered the Baltic opposition movement. The popular fronts that developed quickly—and bravely—raised the question of sovereignty. The Estonian Parliament went the furtherest, proclaiming at an extraordinary session in November 1988 its right to veto laws passed by the Supreme Soviet. The resolution declared all Estonian land, natural resources, and industries the property of the republic.

Gorbachev was furious. To accept the republic's right to veto Moscow's decisions was just as unthinkable as the redrawing of boundaries demanded by the Armenians. Once again the very basis of the empire was being challenged. In a speech to the Central Committee, Gorbachev issued his strongest condemnation of nationalism yet, saying that Estonia's defiance of central power affected the "destiny of our whole union." Estonian land and property, he said, belonged to all Soviet people. "Comrades," he continued, "it would be disastrous, it would put in jeopardy our *perestroika*."

Economic failure

The centerpiece of *perestroika* was economic reform. Yet, in view of the problems facing Gorbachev's government, economic reforms became risky. Bold plans to reinstate private property, for example, were given up because they could not be reconciled with the maintenance of a planned economy and the one-party system. The construction of a free market was indefinitely postponed because it required a fundamental pricing reform, which was certain to cause inflation and result in social unrest. The situation with consumer goods became extremely bleak. Staple foods were in short supply, and even when available were shunned because of saturation with pesticides, nitrates, and other chemicals. There was a sad joke that claimed even Soviet cats snubbed the sausages produced for human consumption.

Countless additional factors contributed to the failure of economic-reform plans. Many scholars emphasize the inherent difficulty of developing private enterprise in a centralized economy.

Soviet citizens did not trust the government to honor promises to respect the rights and earnings of cooperative enterprises. But above all, there were the vested interests of the Party bureaucracy to whom state ownership assured an easy and comfortable living. The bureaucracy feared the political consequences of the accumulation of wealth in private hands. Moreover, *perestroika* aggravated social inequalities in a country where inequalities are poorly tolerated. It also increased unemployment, which is not supposed to exist in a communist state. "Such inequalities and such unemployment, on top of generally declining living standards," wrote one scholar, "create a situation laden with revolutionary possibilities."

Facing the events in Eastern Europe

The collapse of Eastern European Communism shocked the world. Certainly, few supporters or friends of Soviet Communism predicted it. In their view, the countries of Eastern Europe had real governments that were worthy of being treated as if they represented their citizens. But most conservatives always saw these regimes as nothing more than a bunch of thugs who ruled only by the threat of Soviet guns. If ever the threat were lifted, they claimed, the regimes would be swept away in a matter of days. And that is exactly what happened.

Whatever Gorbachev's ultimate intentions for communism were or are, throughout 1988 and 1989 he gave the impression to the Eastern Europeans that Soviet troops would not shoot to prevent even profound deviations from totalitarianism—so long as their countries remained within the Warsaw Pact. In May 1989, when the Hungarian government started to tear down the barbed wire fences along the Austrian border and made it clear that the border police would no longer fire at escapees, Gorbachev did not object. By the beginning of November 1989, when Gorbachev visited East Berlin, crowds chanted his name as a talisman against their own Communist bosses. As the demonstrations in Leipzig mushroomed, Gorbachev let it be known that he had been on the phone with the commander of the 380,000-strong Soviet forces in East

Germany, telling him to keep his troops in their barracks. He allowed the storm to rage.

Nonetheless, the Eastern Europeans were aware of the colossal Soviet military presence in their countries. On December 8, 1989, for example, Hans Modrow of East Germany warned, "Wherever there are weapons it is necessary to understand that there is a limit. Weapons have to be where they belong, and must not fall into the wrong hands." (But, of course, the source of the peoples' grievances was precisely that the weapons *were* in the wrong hands for 40 years.)

In Czechoslovakia, on November 29, even as the Communist party was almost unanimously voting in Parliament to abolish its own guaranteed "leading role" in society, the defense minister made a point of declaring that the army "definitely stands to support the general secretary of the Party." In neighboring Hungary, the defense minister gave an interview to a Western newspaper stating that the Hungarian army remained a faithful member of the Warsaw Pact.

As for Poland, when its anti-communist Prime Minister Tadeusz Mazowiecki visited Moscow on November 24, he felt compelled to rededicate his ferociously anti-Soviet country to continued faithful membership in the Warsaw Pact and to apologize to Gorbachev for widespread incidents in which Polish youth had desecrated Soviet military graves. Much as Mazowiecki and others in the region enjoyed unprecedented freedom and a taste of power, they feared Soviet intervention. In Poland, as everywhere else, "the guns" were in the hands of the armed forces and the police, who for 40 years lived a class apart from the rest of society and who were suddenly more isolated than ever. "The upshot was," wrote one scholar, "that the overwhelming majority of the Eastern Europeans became powerful petitioners, but they were not yet truly sovereign. Over their heads, out of sight, hung the threat of violence—either from domestic or Soviet troops."

One can only speculate about the rationale for Moscow's restrained, open-mined policy in Eastern Europe. The most likely explanation is that Soviet authorities concluded that the economic and social situation in Eastern Europe had become potentially so unstable that nothing short of massive economic aid could prevent an explosion. This help was unavailable. Moscow, with its own domestic problems, had no resources to spare. The alternative was forceful suppression of any unrest, but that would have injured Gorbachev's carefully nurtured image as a liberal man and a man of peace, which he needed to qualify for Western aid.

As the communist system was collapsing in Eastern Europe during the fall of 1989, the Soviet government was losing its authority closer to home. For example, Moscow could do nothing except negotiate with the miners of Vorkuta when they struck in October 1989. On November 7, 1989, the anniversary of the Bolshevik coup, demonstrators carrying anti-communist banners paraded in Moscow and in other cities. In several republics, dissidents disrupted official celebrations on that occasion; in Georgia and Armenia they forced the authorities to cancel them. More ominously, the armed forces encountered open defiance. By 1990, 10 percent of those called for induction failed to show up. In the Baltic republics, draft centers were blocked by protesters. Men in uniform were regularly assaulted throughout the Soviet Union. In 1989, 53 Soviet officers were killed in public assaults.

A changeable role

The Communist party was the dominant player in the Soviet Union, and the Party's general secretary was the effective leader of the nation. That person possessed powers that were unstated and unrestricted by law. With no fixed term of office and no mechanism for succession, he ruled as long as he was able to control the Party's Politburo and the inner circle of the Party's Central Committee. Of the six previous Soviet leaders, only Nikita Khrushchev was ousted during his lifetime; the others managed to remain in office until they died. "Successors," one Soviet explained, "were chosen by intrigue."

In January 1990, Gorbachev tried to transfer political authority from the Party to the government—a delicate exercise that involved reducing the Party's day-to-day administrative role. It also required ending the ban on competing political parties, and establishing a strong presidency. In theory, a complete transition would mean that his real power would be derived from his position as president rather than as general secretary.

As the Party's Central Committee met to discuss these changes, more than one hundred thousand people rallied nearby demanding democratic change. On February 7, 1990, Article Six of the Soviet Constitution was eliminated by the Central Committee. Article Six was the most important building block of the Soviet Union; it was created by Lenin and guaranteed the Party's "leading role." Ever since the rise of the Communist state, the Party's power and influence were taken for granted by two generations of Soviets. Now, it was being pushed back with mind-boggling resoluteness.

In March 1990, Gorbachev became the first *president* of the Soviet Union and was equipped with vast powers. The election took place during an exciting Party Congress. The timing of the Congress increased the jittery feeling that things were coming apart. On its normal schedule, it would not have been convened until summer; Gorbachev called the special session to rush his presidency into law. Furthermore, tensions among the Soviet republics had become acute, making a reassertion of authority in the center seem necessary. In January, Azerbaijani Muslims went from apartment to apartment in their capital of Baku, attacking Armenian Christians and driving them out of their homes. That set off a spasm of ethnic violence with Armenia and a threat of Azerbaijani secession, which prompted Gorbachev to dispatch troops to Baku. Then, in February, rumors that Armenian refugees were getting choice housing ignited riots in the Central Asian republics of Tadzhikistan and Kirghizia. And in March, on the day before the Congress convened, the newly elected Parliament of Lithuania declared the republic independent, causing Gorbachev to open the session with an expression of alarm. Throughout the country, the economy was in chaos. The first round of local elections in the Russian republic, on March 4, showed that the worst liability a candidate could have was a background as a Communist party official, and the most helpful credential that of having been a political prisoner. In fact, independent pro-democracy groups achieved major gains in the Russian, Ukrainian, and Byelorussian republics and outright control of their local governments.

A strong presidency

It was no wonder that many of the deputies who gathered at the Party Congress on the morning of March 12 were ready to support a strong presidency. "There is a fear with deep resonance in Russian history," one historian has written, "where there seemed to be no authority without authoritarianism, no order without oppression, no change without upheaval." That, in his view, was what attracted many deputies to the concept of a strong presidency: "to fill the power vacuum that many felt had consumed the leadership and would soon consume them all."

After several days of debates, Gorbachev achieved the margin of votes needed to become president. Of precisely 2,000 ballots distributed, 1,878 had been dropped into the ballot boxes. (The rest were retained by deputies who favored a general election: They were taking their ballots home to show constituents how they had refused to vote, as a protest.) Of these, 54 were invalid, 1,329 had been cast for Gorbachev (just 59.2 percent of the total membership of the Congress), and 495 were against him. Only minutes after the announcement of his election, Gorbachev inaugurated himself. He had to memorize the oath and swear himself in as the Soviet Union's first president. Interestingly, Gorbachev recited the oath with a significant change that had been made by the Congress. Instead of pledging to "serve the Soviet people," as the original was written, Gorbachev pledged to "serve the peoples of our country," the plural having been inserted to meet the growing sensibilities of the population's diverse ethnic groups.

As a result of Gorbachev's new role, the overall power shifted from the Communist party to government institutions. The deliberate weakening of the Party's role was blatant. The presidential election was handled by two parliamentary institutions that are still learning how to practice democracy: the restructured Supreme Soviet and the Congress of Peoples' Deputies. The Politburo and the Central Committee of the Communist party (the traditional power centers) were not involved. A 16-member Presidential Council was created (the membership is now 17). Except for the chairman of the Council of Ministers, all the members of the Presidential Council were hand picked by Gorbachev. According to several of its members who have explained its operations, this is not an executive organ. Nevertheless, Gorbachev makes a point of seeking advice from the Council, which therefore has significant influence. The president's new governmental practices will lead to a curtailment in the traditional functions of not only the Politburo but also the government itself, that is, the Council of Ministers.

The constitutional amendments that were approved in March by the Party Congress contained the seeds of a pluralistic system. Beginning with the expiration of Gorbachev's current term, in 1995, a president is to be chosen every five years by all the voters in a general election. Only citizens between the ages 35 and 65 may run (Gorbachev will then be 64). No president may serve more than two terms. A succession mechanism, designed to minimize back-room scrambling for power, names the chairman of the Supreme Soviet as next in line and then the chairman of the Council of Ministers. Either would serve for no more than three months; then a new election would be held.

The president may be impeached for violating the law of the constitution by a two-thirds vote of the Peoples' Deputies, which normally meets twice a year. His vetoes of legislation may be overridden by a two-thirds vote of the Supreme Soviet, which also has the power, if it becomes independent-minded, to restrict the president's ability to issue decrees or declare states of emergency. The legislature may vote "no confidence" in the Council of Ministers, requiring its six members to step aside. Article Six was revised to permit the participation of other political parties.

These were momentous changes for a system that never honored the rule of law. For many scholars, these amendments marked the end of communism in the Soviet Union.

Russian secession?

In the Soviet heartland—the Russian republic (officially the Russian Socialist Federative Soviet Republic)—there were also nationalist strivings. Some people even called for Russia's complete secession from the Soviet Union. In May 1990, this demand was voiced by Boris Yeltsin, who garnered praise, but also stiff opposition, from

A striking coal miner from the Kuzbass shouts at a speaker during a rally. The strike, which originated in Siberia, spread rapidly to the country's richest coal-producing area in the Ukraine. (Reuters/Bettmann Archives)

Gorbachev. Yelstin exploited the popular wave of dissatisfaction to promote himself as a super-reformer and as Gorbachev's adversary. He criticized the methods used by Moscow's central authorities, saying they were no longer the route to full independence for the republics.

Members of the new Russian Parliament sat down in early June 1990 to draft a "declaration of sovereignty." They promised that a reformed Russia would guarantee all citizens, political parties, public organizations, and religions "equal legal opportunities for participation in running the affairs of the state and society." The sheer size of Russia, largest of the Soviet republics, is sufficient to boggle the mind. Straddling most of the Eurasian land mass of some 6.5 million square miles, it includes Arctic tundra, Pacific coasts, Volga steppes as well as far-flung settlements in southern Siberia. The Russian republic produces 90 percent of the Soviet Union's oil and 70 percent of its natural gas. It is home to more than 146 million people, who speak some 50 languages. Russia also contains one of the globe's largest collections of nuclear weapons. If it declared independence tomorrow, it would be a world power in its own right.

The real battle for all nationalists, whether Latvian or Russian, is with the center. Gorbachev and his allies are largely ethnic Russians, but they dream about *perestroika* as a process of bringing all the country's parts together in a strengthened socialist federation. Under the twin pressures of nationalism and the mortal weakening of the Soviet Communist party, this vision faded.

Moving toward pluralism—Summer 1990

A second Party Congress, originally scheduled for October 1991, was moved forward to October 1990 and then July 2, 1990. This showed the urgent Soviet need to solve the irritating conditions within the Party. The Party was racked by harsh clashes between reformers and conservatives, the latter led by Gorbachev's adversary, Yegor Ligachov. For months, according to most reports, the most frequent word used in political discussions was *raskol*, or "split" or "dissidence." One reporter said that this new word was used more than "Lenin," whose name had almost always been invoked. In its impact for the future, the July Party Congress was no less important than the Congress that took place in 1956 when Khrushchev launched de-Stalinization. Under Gorbachev's masterly guidance, the July Congress passed resolutions that supported him in every way. A qualified majority reelected him as general secretary and placed his personal candidate, Vladimir Ivashko, a Ukrainian decribed as "rather bland," in the newly created position of deputy to the general secretary.

Boris Yeltsin's dramatic resignation from the Party at the end of the Congress made it obvious that Party conditions can be by no means viewed as peaceful and orderly. Gorbachev wants to "combine a broad democratization [inside the Party] with centralism and discipline." But they have only begun to fight. Not only has *raskol* existed for a long time between the Party and the people, but most scholars think it will continue plaguing the Party internally. A multi-party system can be delayed, but it cannot be stopped. New political groupings formed long ago, and they will evolve into new parties that describe themselves as social-democratic, Christian-democratic, or liberal. The question arises whether this movement toward pluralism, which, as in other Eastern European states, challenges the very right of the Communist party to exist, can proceed peacefully.

Despite obvious inadequacies and contradictions, the positive changes made under the heading of *glasnost* are unmistakable. *Perestroika*, in contrast, was tackled only halfheartedly. As Gorbachev himself admitted, "The right concepts could have been implemented, but the courage was lacking." While aiming to "crack open" Soviet foreign policy, the "new thinking" has heightened domestic problems, especially ethnic and social issues, according to Gorbachev. "Social changes," one scholar wrote, "can develop a dynamic of their own, and the overall effects can defy prediction." For decades, a brutal exercise of power created a massive immobility that was buttressed by "a mentality of forbearance and lethargy"; this made the domestic political climate static, tranquil, and also predictable for Soviet rulers. But today, the call for restructuring demands a more open-minded view of society. As a result, the intended prosperity was inevitably linked with social outrages that are not unknown in the West.

The collapse of communism

"It remains hard to believe," one journalist has written, "that Gorbachev viewed the revolutions without vertigo and even dread." The borders of the Soviet Union were not impermeable to the revolutions in Poland, Hungary, East Germany, Czechoslovakia, and Romania. In fact, in a somewhat limited way, hemmed in by various qualifications, the same process of deligitimization that engulfed Eastern Europe was under way in the Soviet Union. As the ideological legitimacy of communist rule in the Soviet Union crumbled, Gorbachev raced against time to find new underpinnings for his own government. So far, he has gambled on political liberalization, feeling his way toward the creation of quasi-representative institutions such as the revamped Supreme Soviet, and abolishing most of the limits on freedom of speech. But he clings to the Party's "leading role" and the lineage of Lenin. As shortages mount and as the cost of economic restructuring looms ever larger, the walls are closing in on Gorbachev. Soviet citizens, as one writer explained, "free to speak and listen but not wash or eat, may begin to feel that they are living the punch line of a joke."

The patience of the Soviet masses, however, is legendary. If the people were willing to tolerate 30 years of Stalinism in the hope that present sacrifice would yield prosperity, then it is not unreasonable to suppose that they may be willing to give Gorbachev another few years. The Soviet Union and Europe overlap, as Gorbachev keeps insisting with his talk of a common "European House." But the Soviet Union is not Europe. It is haunted by histories and fissures that propel it toward a fate that may be chillingly different.

And in some matters, Gorbachev has made it abundantly clear that he is not a reformer at all. His willingness to tolerate the dissolution of the Eastern bloc is not matched by a parallel willingness to tolerate the dissolution of the Soviet empire. And though he has to concede something here and there, it is hard to imagine him standing by, let alone presiding, while the desire for national independence spreads.

Pronunciation Guide

The following names are spelled phonetically and are intended to serve as a guide to pronunciation. Capital letters indicate stressed syllables.

Poland

Zbigniew Bujak   zbig NEE yev   BOO yak
Wojciech Jaruzelski   VOY chek   ya roo ZEL skee
Czeslaw Kiszczak   CHESS waf   KISH chak
Tadeusz Mazowiecki   ta DAY oosh   mah zov YETS skee
Mieczyslaw Rakowski   MYEH chi swaf   rah KOV skee
Florian Siwicki   FLOOR ee an   she VITS skee
Lech Walesa   lek   vah WEN sah

Hungary

Jozsef Antall   YOZH eff   AHN tall
Karoly Grosz   KAH roi   gross
Janos Kadar   YAHN osh   KAH dar
Imre Nagy   EEM re   nahzh
Miklos Nemeth   MEEK losh   NEH met
Imre Pozsgay   EEM re   POHZH gay
Matyas Szuros   MAHT yash   SOO rosh

East Germany

Erich Honecker   EHR ik   HOH nek ker
Helmut Kohl   HEL mut   kohl
Egon Krenz   EGG on   krents
Lothair de Maiziere   LOH tair   deh MAY zair
Hans Modrow   hans   MOH drov
Gunter Schabowski   GOON ter   sha BOFF skee

Czechoslovakia

Ladislav Adamec   lah DEE slav   a DAM ets
Jan Carnogursky   yahn   char no GOR skee
Jiri Dienstbier   YEER zhee   DEENST beer
Alexander Dubcek   ahl eks AN der   DOOB chek
Vaclav Havel   VAHTS lahv   HAH vel
Gustav Husak   GOO staf   HOO sak
Milos Jakes   MEE losh   YAH kesh

Romania

Silviu Brucan   SIL vyu   BROO kan
Nicolae Ceausescu   NEE ko lai   chow SHEH skoo
Ion Iliescu   yohn   ee lee ESS koo
Dumitru Mazilu   doo MEE troo   ma ZEE loo
Laszlo Tokes   LAHZ loh   TOH kesh

Soviet Union

Leonid Brezhnev   LEH o need   BREZH nyeff
Mikhail Gorbachev   mee kha EEL   gor bah CHOFF
Nikita Khrushchev   nee KEE tah   kroosh CHOFF
Yegor Ligachov   YEE gor   lee gah CHOFF
Boris Yeltsin   boh REES   YELT seen

Glossary

alliance A close connection or friendship between two or more governments, often made by formal, written pact or treaty.

capitalist economy A type of economy in which individuals, not the government, own industries.

Cold War A term used to describe the tensions that developed after World War II between the democratic nations of the West and the Soviet Union.

communism A political and economic system in which the government owns or controls all property and industry.

general secretary The leader of the Communist party.

de-Stalinization The process of removing Stalin's strict and oppressive controls.

dictator An absolute ruler, especially one who suppresses a democratic government.

dictatorship A government in which a person or small group of people has complete power to rule.

empire A group of lands and people under one government.

ethnic group A group of people who share a language and similar customs.

free enterprise In a capitalist economy, the freedom to own property and run a business largely free of government control.

land redistribution The taking of land from large landowners in order to give it to landless farmers.

market economy An economy that is based on profit and private enterprise.

martial law Military rule.

nationalism A feeling of intense loyalty and devotion to one's country.

nationalize To place control or ownership of an industry in the hands of the national government.

NATO   (North Atlantic Treaty Organization) A mutual defense alliance established in 1949 among Belgium, Canada, Denmark, France, Great Britain, Iceland, Italy, Luxembourg, the Netherlands, Norway, Portugal, and the United States and later joined by Greece, Turkey, and West Germany; its aim was to safeguard the Atlantic community, particularly against Soviet aggression.

privatization   The process of turning state-owned industries into private hands.

politburo   The Communist party's policy-making and executive committee.

Securitate   Romania's secret police.

socialism   An economic system in which land and industry is controlled by the government rather than by individuals or private companies.

Stasi   East Germany's secret police.

totalitarian   A government that controls all aspects of peoples' lives; totalitarian governments are led by a dictator or a small group of people.

tsar   The supreme ruler of Russia until the Russian Revolution and the birth of the Soviet Union.

tyranny   Despotic or cruel exercise of power.

Warsaw Pact   (or Warsaw Treaty Organization) A mutual defense alliance established in 1955 among Albania, Bulgaria, Czechoslovakia, East Germany, Hungary, Poland, and the Soviet Union; it was the Soviet bloc's equivalent of NATO.

zomos   Polish police guards who used violence to break up demonstrations during martial law.

For Further Reading

Eastern Europe has long been a favorite topic for historians, political scientists, and sociologists. Consequently, there is an abundance of material written about it. The following is a sampling of texts related to the rise and fall of communism in the region.

Poland

Ascherson, Neil. *The Struggles for Poland.* New York: Random House, 1987.

———. *The Polish August: The Self-Limiting Revolution.* New York: Viking Press, 1981.

Brumberg, Abraham (ed.). *Poland: Genesis of a Revolution.* New York: Vintage Books, 1983.

Davies, Norman. *God's Playground: A History of Poland.* London: Oxford University Press, 1981.

Michnik, Adam. *Letters from Prison and Other Essays.* Berkeley: University of California Press, 1985.

Weschler, Lawrence. *The Passion of Poland, from Solidarity through the State of War.* New York: Pantheon Books, 1982.

Hungary

Barber, Noel. *Seven Days of Freedom: The Hungarian Uprising.* New York: Stein & Day, 1974.

Hoensch, Jorg. *A History of Modern Hungary, 1867–1986.* London & New York: Longman, 1988.

Gati, Charles. *Hungary and the Soviet Bloc.* Durham, N.C.: Duke University Press, 1986.

Nagy, Imre. *On Communism: In Defense of the New Course.* London: Thames & Hudson, 1957.

Rupnik, Jacques. *The Other Europe: The Rise and Fall of Communism in East-Central Europe.* New York: Pantheon Books, 1988.

East Germany

Childs, David. *The GDR: Moscow's German Ally.* London: George Allen & Unwin, 1983.

Dornberg, John. *The Other Germany.* New York: Doubleday, 1968.

Tusa, Ann. *The Berlin Blockade.* London: Hodder & Stoughton, 1988.

Wyden, Peter. *Wall: The Story of Divided Berlin.* New York: Simon & Schuster, 1989.

Czechoslovakia

Havel, Vaclav. *Living in Truth.* London and New York: Faber & Faber, 1987.

———. *Letters to Olga.* New York: Alfred A. Knopf, 1988.

Levy, Alan. *So Many Heroes.* Sagaponack, N.Y.: Second Chance Press, 1980.

Nyrop, Richard. *Czechoslovakia, A Country Study.* Washington, D.C.: American University, 1982.

Skilling, H. Gordon. *Czechoslovakia's Interrupted Revolution.* Princeton, N.J.: Princeton University Press, 1976.

Romania

Ash, Timothy Garton. *The Uses of Adversity: Essays on the Fate of Central Europe.* New York: Random House, 1989.

Dawisha, Karen. *Eastern Europe, Gorbachev, and Reform.* Cambridge: Cambridge University Press, 1990.

Ionescu, Ghita. *Communism in Romania.* London: Oxford University Press, 1964.

Keefe, Eugene. *Area Handbook for Romania.* Washington, D.C.: American University, 1972.

Soviet Union

Cohen, Stephen (ed.). *Voices of* Glasnost: *Interviews with Gorbachev's Reformers.* New York: W.W. Norton, 1989.

Frankland, Mark. *The Sixth Continent: Mikhail Gorbachev and the Soviet Union.* New York: Harper & Row, 1987.

Thompson, John. *Russia and the Sovet Union.* New York: Charles Scribner & Sons, 1986.

Nahaylo, Bohdan, and Victor Swoboda. *Soviet Disunion: A History of the Nationalities Problem in the USSR.* New York: The Free Press, 1989.

Walker, Martin. *The Waking Giant.* New York: Pantheon Books, 1986.

Westoby, Adam. *The Evolution of Communism.* New York: The Free Press, 1989.

INDEX